# AMERICAN WOMEN
# WHO SCORED FIRSTS

## by Aylesa Forsee

This bright adventure into the lives of ten famous American women brings clear proof that one doesn't have to be born under a lucky star to achieve success. Integrity, courage, self-discipline and plain hard work—these are the magic ingredients. And in the face of failure each of these women continued to cherish her dream. Katharine Cornell, for example, fought an almost insurmountable shyness before developing the stage presence which made her a great star. Yet all of them in their upward struggle remain warm and compassionate human beings.

The author has emphasized the dedication and singleness of purpose with which each pursued her career and a summary is given of the qualifications one must have to follow such a vocation.

None of those included in the following pages ever stopped trying. Each faced a hurdle and overcame it with the same outstanding courage. At times all of them stumbled and seemed lost, but within them was the power no chemist or soul-searcher can define: a power which will keep them forever in the history of American life.

You will be glad to know them better.

AMERICAN WOMEN WHO SCORED FIRSTS

# AMERICAN WOMEN
## *who scored firsts*

## AYLESA FORSEE

Macrae Smith Company: Philadelphia

# CONTENTS

# CONTENTS

# FOREWORD

The women whose lives are set forth in this book were not born under a lucky star, nor did they possess some magic charm. No two of them arrived at success by the same route. Each had a unique combination of qualities. Yet certain attributes were common to all—integrity, courage, self-discipline, greater than average willingness to give of their talents and of themselves.

And they knew what they wanted. There was no vacillating from one desire to another, no starting one project with enthusiasm and eagerness only to drop it for something that looked more promising. They wanted what they wanted more than anything else in the world. Even when the going was rough they cherished the dream, the vision, the beauty that had formed in their minds. Having attained one degree of excellence they continued to set themselves new standards. They accepted the responsibility for developing the gifts which had come to them from a Power beyond themselves and turned them into beauty.

# AMERICAN WOMEN WHO SCORED FIRSTS

# 1: MARIAN ANDERSON

## Grace Before Greatness

In the fall of 1954 the Metropolitan Opera Company announced that Marian Anderson was under contract to sing in Verdi's *The Masked Ball*. Immediately reporters swarmed around the famous contralto, first Negro singer ever to appear with a Metropolitan cast.

"I'm very happy," Miss Anderson told the newspapermen.

"Give us a smile to prove it," said one of the photographers.

Miss Anderson smiled, but added, "The happiness is inside."

The distinction of being the first Negro woman to establish herself in the concert world and to win world-wide acclaim did not come to Marian Anderson through a series of lucky breaks. To perfect her gift of song took patience, persistence and selfless devotion.

Marian was born in South Philadelphia in a room her parents had rented when they were married. Later the family, augmented by Alyce and Ethel, moved to a house on Colorado Street. Marian's father worked hard at the Reading Terminal Market and also as a dealer in coal and wood, but could provide very little in the way of luxuries.

Gravely Marian helped her soft-spoken mother, who had been a schoolteacher before marriage, to keep a spotlessly clean house and to care for her younger sisters. But there was plenty of time for play, too. With the thought that she might some day become a surgeon, Marian bandaged and rebandaged her dolls. She loved playing games with Ethel and Alyce, but one of her favorite alone games was la-la-ing to herself while she beat out a make-believe accompaniment on a bench.

As soon as the girls were old enough the Andersons enjoyed singing together—hymns, spirituals, old American songs. A day looked forward to was the annual outing at the Barnum and Bailey circus. The expedition included a ride on a trolley car and a picnic lunch.

Even before she was six Marian attended Union Baptist Church regularly. She was proud of her good-looking father who frequently served as usher. Soon Marian was enrolled in the junior choir of that church and felt very important when the choir leader asked her and a little friend to sing "Dear to the Heart of the Shepherd" as a duet for a church service.

Mrs. Anderson saw to it that school was taken seriously, but Marian, who was haunted by every wisp of song she heard, found it hard to pay attention to her teacher when music classes met in the room next door. Through listening she learned the songs taught in the grade ahead of her —although not always accurately, as in the case of "Peacefully Sleep," which through the wall had sounded like "Sleep, Polly, Sleep."

The day a second-hand piano came into the Anderson home was a gala one. Its arrival was heralded by neighborhood children shouting, "The Andersons' piano is here!" Ecstatically, Marian ran experimental scales. Although there was no money for lessons, she eventually learned to play simple accompaniments through use of a card marked with notes that could be set up back of the keys.

Interest in piano palled after Marian heard a violin played. Knowing her parents couldn't afford an instrument—not even a $3.98 one she'd seen displayed at a pawn shop—she set out to earn the money for herself by running errands and scrubbing doorsteps for the neighbors. Finally she accumulated the required sum and made a trip to the pawn shop with an older cousin. Handing the shop owner a handful of nickels and dimes warm and moist with her excitement, she asked, "Is this a real good one?"

A friend taught Marian how to tune the instrument and play a scale, but one string after another broke and finally the violin was a wreck.

Marian's tenth year was burdened by tragedy. Following a head injury, Mr. Anderson became ill. Shortly after Christmas he died.

The family moved to the home of Mr. Anderson's parents. Their house was large but overflowed with an aunt, two cousins and a number of children receiving day care. Tall, impressive Grandmother Anderson loved children and was sympathetic with Marian's singing, but was rather strict and dictatorial. To earn their livelihood Marian's mother, always valiant and uncomplaining, worked sometimes away from home, sometimes taking in laundry.

By the time she was ready for high school Marian knew she wanted to study music, but she also knew that she needed to get a job as soon as possible. Although she disliked the prospect of becoming a stenographer, she enrolled in a commercial course at William Penn High School. However, after she had sung for an assembly program, the principal recommended a transfer to South Philadelphia High School for its musical advantages.

Marian's interest in musical activities at South Philadelphia High was strong but it did not exclude other things. When the Camp Fire Girls, of which she was a member, were rehearsing for a show, she became enchanted with ballet, dreaming night after night of her prowess in executing pirouettes and arabesques. She even procured a pair of ballet slippers but, unable to afford lessons, she soon lost interest in dancing. Other diversions were big family dinners, spelling bees, speech contests and social activities at the church. After she became a member of the senior choir at her church, the director gave her every possible opportunity to develop her natural talent. She worked hard memorizing all four parts of every anthem. If a soloist failed to appear, Marian could always take over, even singing the bass part an octave higher if necessary.

At the Union Baptist Church there was a big concert once a year, and the soloist most often engaged was Roland Hayes. Interested in Marian's progress, he made valuable suggestions. As soloist, Marian appeared at schools, churches, YWCA's and YMCA's. Once in a while there was a fee. At first this was never more than two dollars, but eventually she was able to establish a minimum of five dollars. Opportunities to sing in other cities, some of which were made possible by Roland Hayes, opened up for her. These trips, which occasionally kept her out of school for several days, meant extra studies and make-up examinations when Marian returned to classes.

As a child Marian had just let herself go, singing naturally and exuberantly, but now musicians who noted the remarkable quality and range of her voice pointed out the necessity of channeling and directing it. This would require lessons. Where was the money coming from, Marian asked herself anxiously.

For a time the need was met by a soprano, Mary Saunders Patterson, who offered her lessons free of charge. But then Marian began to long for a well-rounded formal education available only in a music school. Mrs. Anderson sympathized with Marian's desire, but she had to spend most of her hard-earned money to clothe and feed the three girls. However, she encouraged Marian to find out what the tuition would be. For this information Marian visited a school of music at the beginning of a term, and with rapidly beating heart took her place in a line of students who were registering. Suppose she could afford lessons—what would her teacher be like?

When it came Marian's turn to be handed an application blank, the young employee ignored her, turning to the next student in line. When there was no one left, the employee finally asked, "What do *you* want?"

After Marian had explained that she merely wished to make inquiry about fees the girl told her, "We don't take colored."

Blinded by tears, Marian turned and stumbled out of the conservatory. Gentle by nature, she had been taught by her mother that God never asks who you are. How, she thought, in this place where the beauty of music was all around, could anyone be so cold and unfeeling?

Despite the sting of rebuff, Marian kept on singing and practicing, gaining in poise and graciousness. Her accompanist and manager Billy King arranged long and longer tours for her. Her mother also went with Marian to colleges, churches and clubs in southern cities.

Shortly before she was to graduate from high school Marian's principal, Dr. Lucy Wilson, took her to audition for Giuseppe Boghetti. The stocky, stern-looking Boghetti, who had a waiting list of pupils, was gruff and forbidding at first, but after hearing Marian sing he agreed to make a place for her at once. Marian's exultation collapsed when

[13]

he stated his fee. Never imagining that any amount of money would come to her except through expenditure of her own effort, she gave up the idea of lessons with Boghetti. What Marian didn't count on was the love and confidence her church and community held for her. Hearing of her disappointment, Union Baptists began hoarding their pennies to start The Fund for Marian Anderson's Future. Through sponsoring benefit concerts, church auxiliaries raised five hundred dollars. And when Marian graduated from high school, the Philadelphia Choral Society presented her with a scholarship. Later a continuance of lessons was made possible through a fund provided by the National Association of Negro Musicians.

Boghetti exposed faults in Marian's singing and set her to work on scales, breathing, placement of tones, vocal exercises. With his magnetic quality he taught her that there are no short cuts in achieving true professionalism. "You must learn to do your job under any circumstances," he told her. "You can never say, 'Tonight I don't feel well and I won't appear.'"

During the months she was studying so intensively Marian managed to hear a few concert artists. Their skill in foreign languages made her aware of her own language deficiencies, particularly in German. Meanwhile appearing with groups outside Philadelphia, headlining festivals, cantatas, plays, pageants, Marian was gaining recognition.

Study with Boghetti enlarged Marian's capacities; she had better control. The time had come, she thought, when she could risk a recital at Town Hall in New York. Boghetti helped her plan the program and she worked hard.

It was just too wonderful to be true, Marian told herself on the night of the concert as she watched the clock expectantly. Half-dazed with excitement, she couldn't

[14]

resist peeking out through the curtains. Sponsors had assured a full house. Actually the hall was only half full. To a person of Marian's sensitivity this was a great shock. Onstage, when Billy King went to the organ to accompany her first number, Marian felt miserably alone. Her whole program limped.

Next morning comments of the critics were far from complimentary. "Sang her Brahms as if by rote," said one.

The fact was that Marian just wasn't ready for the debut from the standpoint of either her experience or her maturity, but she saw no excuse for herself. She had worked hard and dreamed high—now she had failed, musically and financially. "I'd better forget all about singing," she told her mother. What hurt the most was her feeling that she had let people down, people who had faith and confidence in her.

"Pray about it," Mrs. Anderson advised.

But Marian, full of doubt and indecision, didn't follow her mother's advice. Convinced that she could never become a great musician, she appeared only intermittently at Mr. Boghetti's studio and turned down the few concert offers that came her way.

A comfort in the succeeding weeks of darkness and discouragement lay in the fact that the family was now living in their own little home. In this refuge, fortified by her mother's strength, Marian began once more to feel challenged to give her best.

One day the thought shook her like a gust of wind that only through using the gift God had given her would she ever find happiness and fulfillment. "I want to study again," Marian told her mother. "I want to be the best, and be loved by everyone."

Mrs. Anderson was delighted and gave Marian all possible support, but she also impressed upon her the idea that humbleness comes before greatness. "Prayer begins where human capacity ends," she admonished.

With new determination, Marian resumed her study of music and languages. From Boghetti she got a good background of Italian, and from a French teacher she learned some French. With Billy King, she resumed concertizing.

When Mrs. Anderson, who had a job at the Wanamaker store, began showing excessive fatigue, Marian insisted that she could now earn enough so her mother wouldn't need to work.

In 1923 Marian won a contest for soloists sponsored by the Philadelphia Philharmonic Society. Two years later she went with Mr. Boghetti to Aeolian Hall in New York to enter a contest under the auspices of the Lewisohn Stadium concerts. It was a hot day and Marian's uneasiness became more acute when she saw the auditorium was full of contestants, teachers and accompanists. Almost sixty contestants preceded her. The judges, who sat in the balcony and had begun to look bored, had a noisy clicker. When it sounded a contestant must walk off stage even if in the midst of an aria.

After what seemed hours Marian finally was called to the stage. As she sang she listened apprehensively for the sound of the clicker, but it never came. She was one of sixteen chosen for the semifinals. This audition, which was held later, proved to be an ordeal because of an ear infection Marian had acquired while trying to learn to swim. The judges let contestants leave without indicating how they had fared. Marian and her teacher went to Mr. Boghetti's studio, hoping some word would come before they had to take a train for Philadelphia.

When the telephone jangled Marian jumped up tensely.

"We have won!" Mr. Boghetti shouted as soon as he had hung up the receiver. "There will be no finals."

As the Lewisohn Stadium concert date neared, Marian was very excited. August 26, 1925, family, friends and well-wishers heard her sing several spirituals and "O mio Fernando" from Donizetti's *La Favorita* with dramatic force and naturalness. Marian made an excellent impression on the critics.

After that bookings for concerts were a little more readily obtainable, and fees were higher, too. Marian made a few recordings and received offers from several concert agencies. But there were more obstacles than she had anticipated. Expenses were high on tours, and there weren't so many engagements as Marian had hoped for. In many places where she sang she could not get a room at a hotel. To make matters worse, concert manager Arthur Judson raised the question as to whether Marian should continue as a contralto or switch to soprano.

Nevertheless, Marian had most of the attributes a girl aspiring to a career in music ought to have. She was intelligent, had a good personality and extraordinary talent coupled with artistic sensitivity. Audiences responded well to her, and she'd had more experience with choral groups than most young singers. The prospect of hard work didn't bother Marian, for laziness and self-indulgence which kill many careers had no part in her make-up. Her goal was not glamour or income. She simply had an overwhelming need to use her gift and a keen sense of responsibility about perfecting it. But gradually Marian realized that in addition to all the usual difficulties of getting established in a highly competitive field, she had the added drawback of color. No matter how enthusiastic managers might be, promoting a Negro contralto was far from easy.

Once more Marian became discouraged. Music was her prime interest, her heart's desire, but her place in American musical life seemed very insecure. Engagements were stalemated, old vocal faults remained uncorrected. Needing a fresh impetus she discussed with her family the possibility of going to England to study with Raimund von zur Mühlen. If she lived very modestly it could be managed, the family decided.

Marian's visit to England began inauspiciously. In London the person to whom she had a letter of introduction had gone to a nursing home, leaving no message for her. During the confusion of finding a place to stay Marian lost her music case, which contained not only valuable songs but travelers' checks and important personal items. But with the help of John Payne, once a house guest at the Anderson home, Marian recovered her music case at the Lost Property Office in the Paddington Station.

A new crisis confronted her when, after only two lessons with Raimund von Zur Mühlen, she was told that he was ill and would be unable to continue his work. As an alternative Marian studied in turn with several teachers in London. Although busy and happy to be doing what she wanted to do, she was often homesick.

Financial limitations made it necessary for her to return home at the end of the year. What she had gained was not readily apparent and did little to stimulate her bookings.

After a series of concerts Marian once more felt the need for further European study. This time, because she wanted to work on German lieder in the country of their source, she chose Germany. Encouragement came in the form of a fellowship provided by the Rosenwald Fund. Marian had no acquaintances in Berlin and no satisfactory background of German. But she had her music. Because her sole ambition was to do her best, she disciplined herself into settling down to a relentless routine of practice and study.

Seeking simplicity rather than glamour, Marian concentrated on lieder and the Negro spirituals which had echoed in her since birth. Deeply sensitive to the faith, humility and hope expressed in the songs of her own people, she sang them with touching sincerity.

After a small concert in a school in Berlin, a Norwegian manager and Finnish pianist Kosti Vehanen, who were looking for new talent, invited Marian to tour the Scandinavian countries. Meanwhile she sang a full-length program in Berlin. Apprehensive as to how her group of songs in German had been received she scanned the papers anxiously the next morning. There was not one word about the concert. Berlin critics, she found later, often withheld reviews for several days. In the end most of the comments were favorable.

A short time after this Marian set off for her Scandinavian tour. Kosti Vehanen became her regular accompanist. Although her earnings were modest, Marian gained encouragement and added incentive from the warmth of audience response.

At the end of six months Marian returned briefly to the United States, embarking for Europe again in 1933. This time she stayed two years under Helmer Enwall's management, spending much of her time in Scandinavia where she added a number of native songs to her repertoire.

Audiences loved the deep tragic feeling so predominant in Marian's singing and the way she sang their own songs. Halls were not half large enough to accommodate all who wanted to hear her. There were instances of people waiting all night in line to get tickets.

After a concert in Helsinki there was such a crowd outside the concert hall that it was almost impossible for Marian and Kosti to get to the car, and her black lace dress was badly torn.

Marian was one of the few musicians ever to be invited to the home of the great Finnish composer, Jean Sibelius. Arriving at his villa, she and Kosti found the salon, with furniture done in gold and white, lighted as if for a festive occasion. The sharp-eyed, well-groomed Sibelius and his wife, a beautiful woman with rich, gray hair, greeted them cordially.

Calmly, Marian sang one of Sibelius' songs with a German text, "Im Wald ein Mädchen singt" and several other pieces. Sibelius was enthusiastic. "My roof is too low for you," he told her.

An informal conversation followed in which Sibelius talked about music, his life and career, and Marian told him about America and her family.

The concerts went on and on. The president of Finland told Marian her voice was magnificent. Later she sang before King Gustav in Stockholm and King Christian in Copenhagen.

Enchanted by Scandinavia, Marian spent several vacations there. Summering with the Enwalls on an island off the Swedish coast, she greatly enjoyed the sea, sailing and fishing. But even on vacation she never let herself forget that music had first place in her life, and she never neglected her practicing.

One of the highlights of the subsequent months spent in Scandinavia was a Swedish Christmas. Wearing a warm fur cap, Marian was as delighted as a child riding in a sleigh with snow scrunching under the runners to a little white church with high gabled roof and candlelight.

Between tours Marian worked with several different teachers in France and Germany who helped her gain in flexibility and control. And because she wanted to be able to perform folk songs in their native tongues she mastered French as well as the Scandinavian languages.

Compared with Scandinavia's reception of Marian's concerts, London's was cool. Going on to Paris she was greeted by audiences that fairly bulged the sides of the concert hall. For a young artist, Marian had unusual poise and confidence—her self-consciousness showed only in the use of her hands while singing. But stage fright assailed her temporarily at the Paris Opéra. Dazzled by the gorgeousness of the house and the stunningly dressed, diamond-bedecked audience, she started on stage, then backed off again. Pushing at her hair, she took a deep breath, then calm and poised she walked out a second time. Her singing brought wild applause, and the director of the Opéra assured her that her French diction was accurate and clear.

The real secret of Marian's customary absence of stage fright, bugaboo of so many concert musicians, lay in her conviction that God had given her the gift of song and that He would direct and guide her in the use of it. Then too, Marian never ran the risk of underpreparation, which is often the basis for nervousness among amateur musicians.

While Marian was in Paris, impresario Sol Hurok offered to sponsor her in a series of American concerts. But before her return home she made various appearances in other parts of Europe, including Russia. To a recital in the Mozarteum in Salzburg the summer of 1935 only a few persons came. Mrs. Moulton, an American interested in Marian's career, arranged a private recital. Guests included famous conductors, singers, artists and religious personages.

Notified that Toscanini was in the audience, Marian felt her heart turn flip-flops. At the conclusion of the concert when he congratulated her she was so flustered she didn't hear a word he said. Later a friend repeated his congratulations, "Yours is a voice such as one hears once in a hundred years."

After further appearances Kosti and Marian, eager to see her family and friends, embarked for home to make a scheduled appearance at Town Hall. The sea was rough and Marian slipped on a stairway. As her ankle buckled under her, her first thought was, I wonder if I can do that concert.

In the excitement of homecoming the injury was pretty much forgotten, but next morning Marian's toes had turned blue and green and her foot was numb. At a hospital X-rays showed a break. The cast, the doctor told her, would have to stay on for six weeks.

Her long white dress would hide the cast from the audience, thought Marian, but how could she stand? On the night of the concert she had the curtains kept closed while she was wheeled on stage. Supporting herself in the curve of the piano she not only got along without crutches but managed to appear poised and stately. Singing with her eyes closed, as was her habit, Marian, momentarily forgetting her discomfort, completely captivated her audience by the way her voice caressed both the music and the words.

Remembering the blasts from the critics at her previous appearance at Town Hall, Marian put in some restless hours.

This time, however, the reviews in the morning papers

were rapturous. "Grandeur of interpretation . . . Intelligent musicianship . . . She has returned to her native land one of the greatest singers of our time."

Mr. Hurok was unable to schedule the number of concerts he had planned for Marian—the fact that she was Negro was still working against her. But he had faith in her ultimate success and treated her with tactful consideration.

On her second visit to Russia in May of 1936 a small, friendly man named Tolchinsky was assigned by the government to serve as travel manager. "Toll can do anything," he would say smilingly, using the nickname Marian had given him. He almost did, even to producing shrimp and strawberries out of season.

During the intermission of a concert in Moscow Marian met the distinguished composer Shostakovitch, who looked very much like a young student. Stanislavsky, the elderly and refined director of the Moscow Art Theater, gave a tea for Marian—the tea being served from a large samovar. Impressed by Marian's talent, Stanislavsky invited her to stay in Russia and study *Carmen* with him. Although touched by his offer, she declined.

Because Marian's concerts were given in widely scattered cities, she had to do much of her traveling on the train. On long hops Kosti's pet turtle, whose greatest accomplishment was darting out a red tongue to eat leaves, helped pass the time.

In the various cities where Marian sang, she and Kosti visited theaters and museums, saw ballet, heard opera and ate unusual foods such as caviar and chicken cutlets à la Kiev. Journeying southward, Marian and Kosti found fields of golden wheat replacing snow.

Shortly before they reached Tiflis, Toll had to return

to Moscow. Unacquainted with the language, the city or the people, they were uneasy, but managed to make their wants known. From Tiflis they flew to Baku, famous for its oil. Near the city a storm developed. Marian had visions of landing in one of the yellowish-green pools of oil that looked like some poisonous liquid. The plane did have to make an emergency landing—in mud. As she transferred from plane to auto, her hat blew into a pool of oil, but she got no sympathy from Kosti, who for a long time had been trying to persuade her to buy some new hats.

From Baku, Marian and Kosti headed for the summer resort of Kislovodsk, where as guests of the Russian government they enjoyed resting, hiking, taking mineral baths.

Back in Moscow, Marian felt very rich. Concert fees had been paid in Russian bills of small denominations which were presented to her wrapped in newspapers. The problem was that the money could be spent only in Russia and it was good only in certain stores. On a buying orgy, Marian converted much of her cash into furs, antiques, pearls and diamonds. At the end of the Russian tour, Toll and other friends were at the Moscow station to see her and Kosti off. Stanislavsky sent a lovely basket of white lilacs. Since it was the middle of winter, Marian was deeply impressed.

Gradually the number of American concerts increased and Marian spent more time here than abroad, but she still squeezed in appearances in Europe and Africa. At Dakar, take-off point for South America, she enjoyed the exotic colors of rare fruits and flowers and the performance of a native drum orchestra.

Two days before the ship docked, Marian sang a recital for the benefit of the seamen. In Rio de Janiero she gave concerts, but also found time to view botanical gardens and other points of interest. While Marian and Kosti were at a snake farm one of the deadly reptiles slithered over the wall supposedly confining it and landed close to Marian. Instead of fleeing, she astounded the caretaker by stopping to take a picture.

In Rio and Buenos Aires Marian and Kosti found musical tastes at a very high level. Audiences were enchanted by the *artista* who sang as if she understood their loves and longings.

When Marian returned to America she found eager audiences awaiting her. On the few occasions when she gave indication of being interested in applause or the lovely things people said about her, Mrs. Anderson would remind her, "Grace always comes before greatness."

While Marian was in San Francisco in 1939 she learned that negotiations for use of Constitution Hall in Washington for a concert had bogged down. The Daughters of the American Revolution had ruled that one of her race could not appear there. Newspaper headlines proclaimed that by way of protest Eleanor Roosevelt had resigned from the organization. Statesmen, clergymen, musicians vigorously criticized the D.A.R. action.

Continuing her tour eastward Marian refrained from comment and trusted Hurok to work things out. But she was disturbed by the unpleasantness, and by the time she reached Washington was feeling sad and disheartened.

When an invitation came from Harold L. Ickes, Secretary of the Interior, to sing in the open from Lincoln Memorial on Easter Sunday, Marian disliked the idea because it seemed sensational. But then she saw that her own feelings were of small significance—she had become a symbol of her race; if this appearance would somehow serve her people she wanted to go through with it. In the end her manager Sol Hurok announced a free, open-air concert for lovers of music and believers in true democracy.

On Easter morning with her family and a motorcycle escort, Marian Anderson rode down streets bordered by cherry blossoms to the memorial honoring a man who had devoted his life to freeing her people. Looking very regal and beautiful in a long black velvet dress and mink coat, Marian took her place on the platform bristling with microphones. Behind her sat important governmental officials, congressmen, her mother. In front of her a crowd of seventy-five thousand people stretched in a great semicircle. Marian had never been more deeply moved. She felt an obligation to give a message of peace, brotherhood, understanding, but for a moment she was too choked up to sing. Professionalism came to her rescue. As she sang, all the sincerity and depth of her reverence was in her voice. At the end of the concert there came tumultuous cheers. Millions who were not at the recital heard Marian's voice on radio or saw and heard her on newsreels. A mural commemorating the event was painted in the Department of Interior Building.

That same year Marian was awarded the Springarn Medal, given annually to the Negro who has made the highest achievement in any honorable field of endeavor. And she was invited to the White House to sing for the King and Queen of England when they were guests there. Marian, who had been there before, made her way with all the poise of a princess through the crowd milling restlessly about in the humid weather. She sang superbly. Later her curtsy to the queen, which she had practiced for days, didn't come off so well, but Elizabeth, who looked like a fairy-tale queen in chiffon, sequins and shining jewels, greeted Marian in a friendly, gracious manner.

The next fall, booked for two years in advance, Marian embarked upon a rigorous series of concerts. When illness forced Kosti Vehanen to return to his homeland, Marian employed Franz Rupp as her accompanist. A very talented musician who described himself as a "Yankee mit accent," Franz gave Marian invaluable assistance in the interpretation of German lieder.

Singing to packed houses Marian unfailingly won frenzied applause or the tribute of awed silence. The morning after a concert in Houston, Texas, the Texas *Post* remarked, "If there was a dry eye in the house it was because they sold a seat to a stone man."

Whether her audience was small or large, musicianly or amateurish, old or young, Marian was a perfectionist about her program. "You want to do your level best every time you perform," she told reporters.

Marian's tours were often more taxing to her personal manager Isaac Alexander Jofe than to herself, because she insisted on taking not only the usual necessities, but also a typewriter, tape recorder, electric plate, camera and a sewing machine on which she made items such as slacks, summer dresses and even curtains. Jofe's pleas to travel light brought some reduction in the pieces of luggage. But the typewriter still went along. Marian was always promising herself that by using it she could catch up on her correspondence—personal notes, fan mail, letters ranging from questions as to where she got the dress she wore in Dallas to requests like, "Please send me twenty thousand dollars. I intend to open a flower shop. Will call the shop Marian. It will be good publicity for you." Despite her good intentions, however, Marian's tours usually ended with

[27]

letters unanswered. Anyone she really wanted to communicate with usually got a telephone call. One chat with her mother and sisters cost Marian over fifty dollars.

When not on tour Marian took time to sing on radio and television and to record songs. Because she does not feel at ease while recording, and misses audience response, the process is a chore for Marian. She strives to make recorded songs sound as natural and as nearly perfect in every detail as possible. If she feels she is not up to par after doing one recording she will wait until another time to go on with others.

Generous in her use of talent, she has given benefits for the Red Cross and has sung in hospitals and prisons both at home and abroad. During World War II she appeared at various army camps. After war broke out in Korea she sang in a hospital ship off Inchon, and on shore for battle-weary troops. At one place two young men approached her for autographs. Noticing that they seemed agitated, she mentioned it.

"We went A.W.O.L. for this concert," one of them explained. "And we have to hurry back to the front before we're missed." As generous with material gifts as with her talent, Marian prefers her charities, whether giving crutches to a cripple or a large check to war relief, to remain anonymous. Although she has not done a great deal of public speaking, Marian does an excellent job when called upon. She is clear and straightforward in her presentation.

Polishing and sharing her gift of song has kept Marian too busy to cultivate many close friends, but she is devoted to her family and does many thoughtful things for them. For her mother she insists on becoming clothes and the best of everything, including the books which Mrs. Anderson reads almost incessantly. Marian is also concerned about the welfare of her sister Alyce, who makes her home with Mrs. Anderson, and Ethel, who lives next door.

In 1940 Marian received the Bok Award given annually to a distinguished Philadelphia citizen. She used the money which went with it for a scholarship to be administered annually to help young people, regardless of race, creed, or color, to pursue an artistic career. As the original ten thousand dollars dwindled, Marian added more to it, creating the Marian Anderson Scholarship. Dozens of young singers have already benefited from the fund.

There have been many other awards in Marian's life, including honorary degrees of Doctor of Music from Howard University, Temple University, Smith College and other institutions. Sibelius dedicated his song, "Solitude," to her. Finland presented her with the Order of the White Rose—other foreign governments have heaped honors and decorations upon her.

But favors, applause, spotlights made little difference in Marian's way of life; she has remained gracious, unaffected, modest. On tour she refuses to have a secretary or personal maid and presses her own evening gown before each concert. Marian neither drinks nor smokes. She does splurge on clothes worn on stage, but her street clothes are simple. Although she owns a number of jewels she seldom wears any jewelry except a diamond.

In 1943 Marian married architect Orpheus Fisher, who had been her boy friend in teen-age days. Since his business prevented his accompanying her except on a few tours, Marian cut down on her concert engagements. When apart, the Fishers make frequent telephone calls back and forth.

Marian and Orpheus have a small New York apartment,

but spend as much time as possible at their country place close to Danbury, Connecticut, with a large white frame house, guest house and swimming pool surrounded by rolling hills and fields. Marian likes to get outdoors and is an enthusiastic gardener, growing huge strawberries and exotic flowers raised from seeds gathered all around the world. Because she likes things that respond to attention, Marian checks closely on the progress of various animals on the farm.

Fond of children, the Fishers often entertain their nephews for weeks at a time. Although Marian admits that some women successfully combine homemaking with a career, she has never felt she could.

When the cook has a day off, Marian likes to experiment with recipes of dishes encountered on her tours in foreign countries and may come up with anything from a cheese soufflé to sweet-sour shrimp. Despite indulgence in diversions such as cooking, gardening, watching baseball on television, Marian spends much time with her music while at the farm. With her accompanist, she rehearses regularly the songs which will be presented on her forthcoming tour. Choice of one's next program, she says, is like selecting what to wear from an infinitely varied wardrobe. Always the audience must be kept in mind, but at the same time what Marian sings must be music she can believe in. One of her favorites is the spiritual, "He Has the Whole World in His Hands," because it reminds us that there is a Being who can help us.

Even if a song is an old one it gets the same assiduous preparation as one Marian has never seen before. The way she works a number out makes a good pattern for any aspiring young singer. Having selected a song to add to her repertoire, she first gives attention to the rhythmic, melo-

dic and technical aspects. Then for days she works at finding the inner meaning of the poetry and at discovering a
way to express it honestly. If she can't uncover something
in the song that will touch listeners, or if she can't make
it match the beauty within her, the song is discarded. "I
want people to leave a concert feeling better than when
they came," she explains. As she practices, Marian listens
for quirks or faults that can creep in unless one is constantly alert.

Marian's acceptance of a contract to assume operatic
roles posed many problems, not the least of which were
fusing singing and acting. For her operatic debut at the
Metropolitan Opera House January 7, 1955, Orpheus and
Marian's family were on hand to encourage her. The opera
was *The Masked Ball;* Marian's first appearance was during the second act. As she stood stirring a witch's caldron
she felt a little unsure of herself. Her voice was too soft
and thin on the opening measures, but soon soared to its
accustomed richness and emotional depth. Sitting in
box thirty-five of the Golden Horseshoe, Mrs. Anderson
proudly witnessed the enthusiastic ovation given her
daughter.

Later that year Marian toured Japan, Korea and eight
of the Caribbean countries. In Japan, where her path
crossed Mrs. Roosevelt's, she was impressed by the intense
concentration and immobility of her audiences. At the
royal palace, where Marian sang for the emperor, a court
orchestra, performing on ancient Oriental instruments,
played for her. As she was leaving she received a delicate
hand-carved figurine. Later on a tour of Israel Marian
encountered audiences with an exceptional hunger for
music.

In October of 1956 Marian embarked for Stockholm,

appearing elsewhere in Europe. That same year her book *My Lord, What a Morning* was released. Autobiographical, it is a simple narrative of her experiences told in a way that reflects her gentleness and sincerity.

When in 1957 the State Department needed a good-will ambassador Miss Anderson, with cooperation from the American National Theater and Academy, was dispatched on a forty-thousand mile, seven-country tour of Asia. When she deplaned in Taipei the first question asked her was, "What about Little Rock?" She heard the same query a number of times. Never bitter in her appraisals, she told schoolboys in Kuala, Lumpur, "Things like hate and fear destroy you, restrict you from being the kind of big person you could be."

Believing that spirituals convey the hope of unity and peace, Miss Anderson sang songs like "Go Down Moses" in Korea, China, Formosa, the Philippines. Even when audiences didn't understand the words, the immense sorrow and beauty conveyed by her music and attitude made them glow with a life that cast a spell over her listeners, whether turbaned school children in Malaya or cabinet officers in Saigon. Miss Anderson hugged babies, laughed with mothers and greeted the great with simple dignity.

In Bombay, where she sang with the Bombay City Orchestra, the performance ended in a wild demonstration of affection with a shower of gifts and flowers—a tribute not only to an outstanding musician, but to a person whose charm and humility had captured the imagination of the Indian people. Climax of the Indian tour came when Miss Anderson sang in Freedom Park in front of a Gandhi memorial.

General Alfred Gruenther, who followed in her wake,

commented, "The United States needs more Marian Andersons. She is our secret weapon." A filmed account of the triumphal tour was later televised on *See It Now*. As a result of this highly successful tour she was, in 1958, given the People-to-People Award as the Philadelphian who had done the most during the past year to bring about understanding between America and people throughout the world.

Her meteoric rise from humble beginnings to recognition as a distinguished citizen and world famous contralto seems to impress almost anyone more than it impresses Miss Anderson herself. "I've had a lot of help," she asserts modestly. And she has—from her mother, friends, interested teachers, musicians and manager Sol Hurok. But of great significance was her single-minded conviction that singing was the thing she had to do. She loved music with all her heart. And she was willing to undergo the self-discipline needed to develop her voice. True, she had superb equipment to begin with, but she didn't grow great simply because she had it—she accepted responsibility for the use of it.

Stamina has been another important asset. Under a rugged and taxing schedule of concerts involving almost constant traveling, hurried meals, little privacy, Marian remains unwilted. But back of her remarkable endurance there is more than a healthy body. Not the least temperamental, Marian stays level-headed and serene even in disconcerting or perplexing situations.

At the conclusion of a concert she will autograph program after program with no sign of annoyance. Because of her race Marian has often run into situations which might well cause frustration, annoyance, embarrassment, but she has maintained her dignity and given no sign of bitterness. To meet such situations takes more than tact; it takes courage. When justifiable criticisms have come her way, Marian has exhibited gratitude rather than resentment and she has set about trying to correct the faults whether of voice or personality.

But the big and basic reason for Marian's success has been her faith in God's care and her conviction that if she adheres to the highest standards, she knows the results will be right. Her voice is rich, powerful, dramatic, but audiences are moved less by her vocal qualities than by her intensity—the way she sings from the heart to the heart.

Marian's belief that God guides her in the use of her talent lets something greater than a human self come through in her voice. It is this profound moral beauty which has sustained and lifted millions of listeners and which has brought the comment, "Marian Anderson can turn a concert hall into a temple."

Marian's selflessness shows through in her habit of saying not, "I am giving a concert tonight," but, "We are giving a concert." Marian insists that it is not herself that makes the program possible but the instruments, the music, the composer, the technicians, the accompanist.

A reporter once asked Marian, "What was the greatest moment of your life?" He expected her to say the White House concert for the King and Queen of England, one of her awards or the Lincoln Memorial concert.

But without hesitation Marian answered, "The day I went home and told my mother she wouldn't have to work any more."

The rule Marian's mother gave her of "Grace before Greatness," has served her well. She can be honored as

[34]

much for her sweetness of spirit and the courage to be herself as for her superb singing. Marian Anderson is more than a great singer: she is a great woman, of whom Fannie Hurst has said, "She has not grown simply great; she has grown great simply." President Eisenhower honored her wide human experience and wisdom when, during the summer of 1958, he offered her a new opportunity to serve her own country and the world by nominating her as a United States delegate to the United Nations General Assembly.

## 2: LILLIAN WALD

### *Angel of Henry Street*

Lillian Wald could have spent her life in luxurious surroundings among a family and friends who would have catered to her slightest desire. But because helping people was the guiding star of her life she took nurse's training, then moved to New York's worst slum to give her services to those who most needed them. To make a name for herself was no part of her plan, but in the process of launching New York's Henry Street Settlement House, pioneering in the field of public health and school nursing, promoting social reforms, she won world-wide recognition for her distinguished service to humanity.

There was little in Lillian's childhood to prepare her for the kind of career she chose. Born in Cincinnati, Ohio, on March 10, 1867, she spent most of her childhood in Rochester, New York, where her father, Max D. Wald, descended from an intellectual family of scholars and professional people, was a well-to-do dealer in optical goods.

The Walds were indulgent parents. Neither one of them even mildly disapproved of the activities of their lovely, brown-haired child with eyes like a faun. Lillian's wants, whether for a ruffled dress, a French doll or a trip on a ferryboat, were catered to as soon as she expressed them.

Lillian, her mischievous older sister, and brothers Alfred and Gus, had a happy, privileged childhood full of the excitement of picnics, parties and dancing school. Their grandfather, Goodman Schwarz, whom they called Favey, not only told them stories more exciting than the *Arabian Nights,* but was always providing candy, treats and ponies to ride. He took the children to the theater and to concerts, built them a bowling alley and taught them how to roll the heavy balls. On long walks he shared their interest in birds and animals and added to their appreciation of the beauty and wonder of the world around them. For the childrens' playhouse, Favey made child-sized furniture. There was even a real stove in the kitchen.

Although Lillian had many privileges, Favey and her Jewish parents, who had left Germany in protest against loss of freedom in the uprisings of 1848, insisted on respect for the rights of others. Giving of oneself as well as of possessions was as natural to the Walds as breathing. Lillian was a very sensitive child, and if people around her were unhappy she wasn't happy, either.

It was Favey who encouraged her interest in the books which were so numerous in the Wald home. But it was her handsome Uncle Samuel Schwarz who developed her love for music and the theater. Lillian, a very imaginative child, had no trouble acting in home-coached plays. Long passages from Shakespeare were declaimed with enthusiasm.

Quite frequently people who had become famous were guests at the Wald home. Perhaps the visitor Lillian liked best was General Sherman who took her for a carriage ride behind army mules.

At Miss Cruttenden's Day School in Rochester, Lillian was a quick, perceptive student, but she was always gay and fun-loving. When she was only fifteen she begged her

[37]

parents to let her go to Vassar. Mrs. Wald, whose fondest dream was a brilliant marriage for Lillian, protested. "How can you have a debut if you're in college?" she questioned anxiously. She did make inquiry, but the president decided Lillian was too young and advised her to apply later. Seeing no alternative, she continued at Miss Cruttenden's, but found the routines a little dull.

Lillian's personal plans were put aside when word came that her brother Alfred had been drowned in California. Alfred had been more than a best-loved brother. With him she had shared the dream of becoming a doctor. Knowing how keenly her parents felt the loss of their son, Lillian concentrated on trying to be a loving, obedient daughter. Just when she was about to revive her cherished plan for Vassar, her sister Julia married Charles P. Barry and Lillian stayed home to ease the loneliness of her parents.

Graduation at Miss Cruttendon's was a major social event. Shortly after that the coming-out parties began. Talented, vivacious, stunning, especially in a satin evening dress, Lillian enjoyed the parties and had more than her share of moonlight and roses. But the deeper she got into the social whirl and the decorous calls with her mother, the more restless she became. There must be some work she was meant to do, thought Lillian, and it was time she was getting at it.

For a while she served as correspondent—the work could be done at home. But Lillian preferred working with people, and she soon became bored with stocks and bonds. What she wanted was a job that would be an outlet for her tremendous drive to help others.

It was while she was on a visit at her sister Julia's summer home at the seashore that Lillian became interested in nursing. Watching the gentle, competent nurse who was called when Julia became ill, Lillian realized here was a profession that would take her out into the world and satisfy her need for service.

Back home, Lillian's announcement that she intended to become a nurse was met by a storm of protest. Who ever heard tell of a girl who was able to marry a handsome, well-to-do husband and live a secure life choosing nursing! In the 1880's girls from cultured homes just weren't supposed to have careers. But knowing that the Walds never denied their children anything they really wanted, Lillian persisted and finally won consent to put in an application at New York Hospital.

Despite her courageous stand at home, Lillian had misgivings as she hurried up the hospital steps for her interview. In the small, high-ceilinged hospital office where she was confronted by brisk, plainly dressed Irene Sutliffe, Director of Nurses, Lillian felt too tall and overdressed. Occasionally Miss Sutliffe looked up from Lillian's application on the desk and fixed her with an appraising eye. Then right in the middle of routine questions, she asked abruptly, "What makes you think you'd be a good nurse?"

Lillian hesitated. Evidently she wasn't making much of an impression. But dishonesty wouldn't get her any place. She answered frankly, "I would love helping people. I think I could do the work well."

On August 20, 1889, Lillian took up her duties as a probationer. To a delicately-bred girl the smells of carbolic acid and ether, crowded living quarters and scanty, poorly prepared food were shocking and disturbing. At that time nurses' training included less in the way of lectures, tests, recitations than today. Students learned largely by doing. This meant spending twelve hours a day on duty. Because

[39]

she could visualize what the training would do for her, Lillian didn't resent the long hours or the menial tasks— they were only a part of learning to serve—but she did find it hard to obey all the rules. Independent, headstrong Lillian, who was accustomed to having her own way, found the almost military discipline hard to bear.

Her first rebuke came when she impulsively raided food supplies in the hospital kitchen to prepare a meal for a patient who said he was hungry. Although she made other mistakes, Lillian soon discovered she had a friend in wise, patient Miss Sutliffe, who appreciated Lillian's intelligence, compassion and eagerness to be of use. And patients, realizing that Lillian saw them as persons, not as cases, loved her.

When she was graduated March 31, 1891, Lillian had learned the techniques of successful nursing. She had also learned the necessity of emotional control and obedience to rules.

Lillian intended to go into active nursing, but when her father died she went home to be with her mother. Tiring of what seemed to be a rather useless existence, she got a position as nurse at the New York Juvenile Asylum. In this grim, high-walled place, she was shocked at the scant comforts given to the children. Automatically labeled as truant or delinquent, when the fact was that many of them were simply friendless or neglected victims of cruelty or poverty, they led a miserable existence. For the most part, the underpaid, undertrained staff members showed a callous indifference toward their charges. On more than one occasion Lillian lost her temper when someone tried to block her attempt to obtain decent treatment for a child. It occurred to her that if she had a degree in medicine she'd have more authority and be in a better position to introduce a few needed reforms at the asylum. Lillian resigned at the end of a year.

In the fall of 1892 she enrolled at Womens' Medical College in New York City, which had been founded by Dr. Elizabeth Blackwell and had a female faculty. Lillian plunged into her studies with customary enthusiasm. But in some ways she found her work frustrating. What she was learning didn't seem to be doing anyone any good. All the classroom teachers kept telling the students how much prejudice they would have to overcome as women physicians. When Lillian was asked if she would care to teach a class in home nursing on the East Side, she gladly took time out from lectures and microscopes.

The East Side was a world Lillian had never realized existed—a world of poverty, illiteracy, filth. In the 1890's this slum area was flooded with immigrants, criminals, derelicts. Gangs of boys wearing ragged, ill-fitting clothing played leap frog in the streets by day and at night slept in doorways, packing boxes or pushcarts. Piles of furniture of dispossessed families stood on sidewalks, dingy family washes festooned fire escapes.

The immigrant women who came to Lillian's home nursing classes were mostly ignorant, timid, untidy in appearance. Words like sanitation meant nothing to them. But their pathetic eagerness to learn and their gratitude stirred Lillian's compassion.

One cold, rainy morning in March 1893, just as Lillian was about to leave the East Side classroom, a thin, pale, shabbily dressed child with tear-stained face came up to her. "My mommy is sick," she said, looking up at Lillian with frightened eyes. "Could you come to see her?"

Lillian took the child's hand and went with her over the slippery cobblestones of a dirty street that smelled of garbage and refuse, up a rotting stairway. The squalor of the dingy two-room apartment made Lillian recoil, but she was not repelled by the mother, who was seriously ill, or by the hungry, half-naked children. As she bathed the wretched woman, changed sheets, mopped the floor, she wasn't feeling sorry for herself; she was simply doing what ought to be done. What these people needed was loving care, thought Lillian. Perhaps she could do more for them through her nursing than by going on with medicine. Her classes at Womens' Medical College suddenly seemed very academic and remote. Was there any reason for returning to them? Why couldn't she live among the poor and take care of their sick?

By the time she left the apartment the East Side had claimed Lillian Wald. The puzzling question as to how she could make her life most useful had been answered.

That night aching muscles and smarting hands reddened by strong soap kept her awake. She lay thinking about the East Side. What was needed was some program of public health nursing. But where could she get backing? Then she thought of Mrs. Solomon Loeb, a wealthy woman who had a reputation for giving generously to worthy causes. It was she who had set up the class in home nursing.

Next day Lillian called on Mrs. Loeb. She meant to be calm, but as she talked about what she had seen in the East Side tenement she became excited and indignant.

"You want me to help with the family?" Mrs. Loeb asked.

Lillian shook her head. "No, I . . ." breathlessly she outlined her plan—trained nurses to live on the East Side and work among the forgotten poor.

Mrs. Loeb had a strange look in her eyes, as if she

thought Lillian might be a crackpot. That anyone could make much of a dent in the filth, disease, criminality of the one hundred and ninety thousand people living in foul, overcrowded rooms on the East Side seemed most unlikely. But Lillian had a vision of what could be done. Mrs. Loeb saw the light of faith shining in the warm, dark eyes of the tall, well-proportioned young woman and admired her courage and wide-open outlook. "I'll consider your plan and let you know later," she told Lillian.

Several weeks later Mrs. Loeb worked out a plan for Lillian. She and a nurse friend, Mary Brewster, were to get modest salaries and funds to be used for medicine and food for the sick and destitute. Mr. Jacob H. Schiff, who was a German immigrant and also was Mrs. Loeb's son-in-law, had also become interested in the project.

Finding a place to live proved to be a problem, but Lillian and Mary got temporary quarters at the College Settlement. Here they found young people of similar interests—students who, by living among the poor and sharing their problems, hoped to prepare themselves to help cure the ills of society. The idea of such an establishment was not new. There had been similar experiments in England. And Hull House in Chicago had been launched two years prior to this, but Lillian knew nothing about the settlement idea and was fascinated.

In July of 1893, Lillian and Mary took up their duties, although the families of both girls were worried and dubious about the undertaking. Tramping from one ramshackle building to another, the two nurses visited patients in dark, airless rooms. Crisp uniforms soon wilted. Everywhere they went Lillian and Mary found heart-breaking poverty. In one home water was kept boiling in two covered pots so no one would suspect that the family had no food to cook. It was in situations like this that the nurses doled out some of the money allotted to them. In other places the need might be for medicine, or coal, or ice. So people would feel less like charity cases, the nurses encouraged them to pay for services, even if they could spare no more than a dime.

Evenings Lillian carefully itemized their expenditures: Eggs for Mrs. B. $.25—Coal for Mr. X. $1.00.

In September Lillian and Mary rented an apartment. It was close to an elevated railroad where sooty trains clanged by, but they made the tiny rooms cozy and comfortable.

At first a number of the East Siders resented the nurses. Little knots of people on the sidewalk eyed them with hostility. At the entrance to one tenement house where Lillian knew there was a sick child, she was barred from entering by a burly-looking man who said ominously, "We don't want no do-gooder poking her nose into our business."

Then there was always the problem of a few slovenly or crafty individuals who took advantage of the nurses to get free food or fuel without deserving it. Persons of less courage and determination would have given up, but Mary and Lillian were neither bitter nor resentful.

Although the work was hard, the surroundings drab, the people sometimes ungrateful, Lillian found satisfaction and reward in helping patients regain their health and hope. Not so visible but no less real were the changes in the minds and hearts of those she served. They saw and felt her gentle-hearted love as she squeezed a dirty little hand or smoothed the sheet of a patient's bed. She treated people as people, not as the poor, the dirty or the ignorant. Gifted at seeing the best and encouraging it, she would tell a pale-faced, listless woman, "You cook like an artist."

In touching ways East Siders began to show their admiration, respect and love. Policemen saluted Lillian. Wherever she went a trail of children tagged along talking about ball games played in the street or a stunted geranium being nursed along in a tin can.

One night when Lillian was entering a rowdy neighborhood where toughs sported guns and defied decency, three rough-looking men approached her. Eyes straight ahead, Lillian walked on without quickening her pace. "This ain't a safe neighborhood," one of the men explained apologetically. "We'll walk along." Although Lillian spent several hours with her patient, the men waited outside to escort her home.

Then there was the Chinese laundryman who called her "Heavenly Lady Number One," and the lean, wiry carpenter with "a touch of rheumatism" who made bookshelves for the nurses to show his gratitude for nursing services, and the Negro who paid ten dollars for sick care.

Knowing he could ill afford it, Lillian protested. "My heart tells me ten dollars," the man insisted.

More and more people with pinched, sallow faces and work-worn hands climbed the stairway to the nurses' apartment asking for a pill for their illness or sympathy and advice on some family disaster. It was the only place many of them could go and be offered a cup of tea in cultured surroundings. Realizing the size of the burdens their visitors carried, the two nurses took no steps to prevent invasion of their privacy. Lillian, with deep understanding of peoples' needs, hopes, fears, brought cheer to the discouraged.

She learned to love the East Side. In the midst of dinginess she enjoyed the color and flavor—women with shawls,

Greek and Hebrew signs, men with hand organs, vendors with pushcarts of fruits and vegetables. For the most part she found the people brave, loyal and lovable.

What discouraged her was that frequently after a patient had been nursed to health he or she would become sick again because of overcrowding, overwork or lack of proper food, sunlight and air. She and Mary could give help to only a fraction of those who needed it.

The longer she lived on the East Side the more keenly Lillian realized that the people would benefit from education and recreation as much as from health services. If they had an education they could improve their lot in life and win for themselves a more secure place in society. And if they had adequate recreation it would help lift them out of their drab, humdrum existence. To do what needed to be done a settlement would be necessary—something much more elaborate than any project yet launched in New York.

Winning support was uphill work. Many people were uninterested or callous to the shocking conditions in the slums. Some brushed her off with the remark, "Poverty is unavoidable." Others who firmly believed that immigrants were shiftless and criminally-minded said, "People like that have to suffer."

With both courage and tact, Lillian persisted in trying to make privileged New Yorkers accept their responsibilities. She never resorted to sob stories or sensationalism, but she had a gift for making statistics come alive and making people feel the hunger, the cold, the despair of East Siders. Her eagerness and personal charm were a big asset. One businessman remarked smilingly, "It cost me five hundred dollars to sit next to Lillian Wald at a dinner party."

By late summer of 1895 the nurses had money enough to buy and move into a solidly built three-story house at 265 Henry Street. A group of nurses whose badges read, "Visiting Nurses under auspices of Board of Health," had come with Lillian to Henry House. They had pledged themselves to go wherever there was a need. This pledge took the blue-caped women with little black bags into strange places—to houseboats on the Hudson, to men living in packing boxes. Lillian had no intention of launching a movement. "I just want it to be like Mrs. Murphy taking a bowl of soup to Mrs. Goldstein," she explained.

The idea of public health nursing did not originate with Lillian. Lodges, religious agencies, even cities had previously supplied limited numbers of visiting nurses. But Lillian and her group ironed out confusion and made this branch of nursing a profession. Lillian selected her nurses carefully. She insisted on pleasing personality and compassion, but the nurses must be efficient, too. Girls with a martyr complex or girls who were interested only because they wanted to build up their own self-esteem were flatly rejected. The fact that, even handicapped by slum conditions, Henry Street nurses had a lower death rate among patients than did New York hospitals convinced city officials that Lillian's program had merit.

Once her public health nursing program was well under way, Lillian turned her attention to the development of educational and recreational facilities. Until the wounds of the human spirit, as well as wounds of the human flesh, were healed, she knew the area would remain a festering sore. To uneducated immigrants who spoke only a little English, Lillian taught English and customs and duties of their new homeland. She set up a Mothers' Club to teach women how to cook cheap foods attractively, plan meals, do home nursing. While teaching such courses, Lillian also managed to get across the importance of neat dress, personal responsibility, values. After one such class session one woman said to another student, "It isn't safe to be selfish."

Lillian also launched a club program for boys and girls. Anyone could join. She never asked a boy's religion or cared about his color. No two clubs were alike in organization, rules, programs or goals. In Heroes Club the life of some American hero was discussed at each meeting. A gang of delinquents who at first menaced the Henry Street settlement by acts of vandalism grouped themselves into the Honor Club. Each club was largely self-governing, although a constitution set forth the rights and duties of members. Only when a principle was at stake did Lillian interfere. She was kindly and understanding, but firm in her insistence upon fair play.

Once a club decided to exclude a Chinese boy. Lillian told the members that if they shut out any boy because of race or religion they could no longer meet at the settlement. She also arranged to have a Chinese visitor, Dr. Yamei Kim, speak to the club. The talented, likeable Dr. Kim made the boys see the worth of the individual, regardless of race. After he had spoken, the club voted to invite the Chinese boy to join them. He became a very popular member.

Mixed in with classes and serious club work there was always plenty of fun at Henry House—parties, folk singing, picnics, dances, celebrations of special holidays ranging from St. Patrick's Day to Jewish holidays. Lillian also conducted story-telling hours. Her wit, sense of humor and gift of dramatization brought the children in droves.

Concerned because one youngster didn't know the difference between a crocodile and a cow, Lillian planned trips to the zoo. But that didn't satisfy her. There ought to be some way of bringing cows and children together. She began planning trips to the country; and, so the children would not start off looking like ragamuffins, Lillian begged clothes for them. Later she succeeded in getting a rest home for mothers and a chain of camps where children could swim, hike and live close to the beauty of sky, birds and butterflies. During a hailstorm one little girl on her first visit to the country said, "God's getting awful fresh throwing down those big stones."

"Don't talk like that," her playmate protested. "Almost everyone in our block loves God."

Both in the country and at Henry House, Lillian tried to surround youngsters with the beauty she knew they didn't have at home. The settlement had clean and lovely rooms with good pictures and fresh flowers. When donations of furniture or books came to Henry House, the things that were dingy or frayed were discarded. Children who frequented the place soon shed their harsh ways and imitated the neat dress of their leaders. To a visitor concerned over a gang of noisy, boisterous boys about to enter Henry House, the janitor said, "I don't worry, miss. I see them come in wild and go out gentlemen."

In addition to the clubs, athletic teams were organized. With the increased number of people coming to Henry House, Lillian couldn't possibly know all of them as individuals, but she kept as close touch as possible.

More than once she bought confirmation dresses for Catholic children, although she was Jewish. Even though many of those who came were classed as delinquents, Lillian never gave a child up. But neither did she hesitate to discipline a troublemaker. Almost invariably, because she acted on a basis of understanding and love, she won cooperation. There was soon a noticeable decline in delinquency in the Henry Street area.

Lillian took just as much interest in the problems of the adults. She maneuvered women into housework, men into street cleaning. If a vendor had no money, she would start him off with a cartload of melons to sell.

Eventually Lillian found herself involved in many activities apart from Henry House. Working at white heat, she always resolutely tackled the job at hand, then without pause moved on to the next one that might be waiting. Everything from the odorous fish stalls to fire protection aroused her. If she saw a peddler selling overripe fruit or decayed vegetables, she reprimanded him in no uncertain terms. But she saw that to correct much of what was wrong on the East Side, legislation would be needed. Never one to sit on the sidelines, she took as her motto, "Find out what needs to be done and do it."

Armed with a mass of shocking information, she spoke at civic organizations and turned New York officialdom upside down. Because her battles were against conditions instead of people, she managed to get legislation for cleaner streets, fire protection and garbage removal without making enemies.

When parents complained that some children with contagious diseases went to school and exposed others, while children who had slight ailments were often sent home, Lillian tried to interest the New York Health Department in providing school nurses. Today school nurses are taken for granted, but at the turn of the century Lillian's suggestion was considered radical. To overcome the reluctance of the New York Board of Estimates to vote the necessary funds, she got permission to use one of her own Henry Street nurses in certain schools. This experiment was so successful that the city voted to employ a dozen nurses—the first municipal school nurses in the world.

A newspaper item set Lillian off on another crusade. One morning in 1905 she read that Congress was about to appropriate several hundred thousand dollars to fight the boll weevil. "The government has spent thousands of dollars on hogs, cattle and oppressed scallops. Now it's out to save the cotton crop," she said with flashing eyes. "Why can't they take as much interest in saving our crop of children?"

Then and there, with the help of a brilliant staff worker, Florence Kelley, Lillian outlined a plan for a bureau to work for the welfare of children. A friend, Dr. Edward T. Devine, sociologist, presented the idea to President Theodore Roosevelt, who was enthusiastic and invited Lillian and Dr. Devine to come to the White House to talk about it. However, the bureau was not approved by Congress until seven years later.

Before the bureau got under way, Lillian was already prodding city and state officials to do something about the evils of child labor. The problem was first brought to her attention by a family of white-faced children pasting paper bags in a dark, chilly basement room. None of the children had ever been inside a school or opened a book. Although children were not supposed to work until they were fourteen, Lillian found them in factories doing backbreaking work. Because the schools were overcrowded, truancy laws were not being enforced.

Whenever possible Lillian exposed dishonest employers, but that didn't take care of those children who worked at curling feathers, pulling basting threads or making artificial flowers for perhaps ten hours a day when parents were desperate for money.

Adult workers needed a champion too, Lillian discovered. Although she disapproved of the rock throwing and picketing activities of some labor unions, she did campaign for better factory practices, particularly with regard to safety.

Another of Lillian's crusades had to do with playgrounds. When she went to the East Side, the only available play spaces were on the streets—both dirty and dangerous. The children were shunted from one spot to another by policemen and irate housewives. Lillian saw to it that a playground was provided at Henry House. The yard bordered by wisteria vine on a trellis and ailanthus trees was as much of a novelty to the children as the swings, parallel bars and sand pile shaded by a gay awning. But this helped only a few. Lillian encouraged schools to follow suit. She also enlisted the aid of parents and school children, who contributed their pennies to provide better play space in parks, and she helped organize the Outdoor Recreation League.

In 1910 Lillian made a round-the-world tour enjoying beauty wherever she found it. But she was horrified at the poverty, starvation and slums in some of the richest cities. Although the trip was supposed to be a vacation, she kept looking for new knowledge that might help her in solving problems on the East Side. Everywhere she went she met millionaires, scholars, heads of governments, but always she sought out the peasants, the laborers, the people who were oppressed.

Back in New York, she launched a further expansion of Henry House activities. Gradually classes were added in art, drama, dancing, music. Distressed by the arrival of culture, a small boy said to Lillian, "Oh, lady, we don't have to take piano lessons, do we?" Lillian assured him he was safe.

To the various classes came mothers, laborers, teachers, immigrants, lawyers, boys and girls. To the clubs came a singing boy named Irving Berlin, a joking boy called Eddie Cantor, a piano-playing boy named George Gershwin.

Meanwhile, the idea of public health nursing had taken hold elsewhere in the country. With over a thousand nurses, Lillian and others felt they should be knit together. In 1913 a national conference was held to discuss community responsibilties. The eager and enthusiastic delegates elected Lillian their first president.

Throughout the years, money-raising campaigns continued to be a necessity for financing Henry House projects, but Lillian was never awed by the magnitude of her task. Her combination of persuasiveness and an irresistible smile roused even the complacent to writing checks. And there were several philanthropists, including the Rockefellers and Rosenwalds, who pledged continuing support.

The contributions that Lillian treasured most were from the poor. One night a shabby stranger came to the door at Henry House and asked, "Is this the house that is good to all nations?"

"I think it is," Florence Kelley told him.

"I've brought you this," said the man handing her a crumpled five dollar bill. To make his contribution he had walked miles.

Lillian's book, *The House on Henry Street*, published in 1915, stirred up an even greater interest in her work. In it she set forth some rather grim word pictures of what life was like on the East Side for the underprivileged.

Addition of new clubs and classes meant more staff, more staff meant more housing. By 1915 there were seven houses instead of one, and property worth a half million dollars. They included a library, a savings bank, house-keeping centers, a social hall with meeting rooms, ball-room, dining hall and roof garden, and a Neighborhood Playhouse.

In the playhouse, donated and directed by the Lewisohn sisters, amateurs gave Yiddish plays, Irish plays, folk dances, ballets. Famous professionals performed there. Later expanded into a school of drama, the theater became recognized for its artistry.

One might have thought that with the settlement on such a firm basis, Lillian would have slackened her pace. Instead, she began casting about for a way to have various national groups on the East Side understand each other better, and at the same time to keep immigrants from feeling cut off from their ancestral heritage. Lillian seized every opportunity for staging festivals or pageants that would keep alive folk songs and drama. These also had the effect of giving children of immigrants some pride in the accomplishments of their parents.

World War I temporarily crippled Henry House activities. Because Lillian hated the suffering brought by war she worked for peace practically up to the minute that war was declared. The rumor got started that Lillian Wald was un-American, and the angry story grew to such proportions that some subscribers to the Henry Street Fund withdrew their support. Lillian knew the charges were false, but she made no attempt to defend herself.

As soon as it became clear that war could not possibly be avoided, she did everything possible to help out. Her nurses were among the first to go overseas. Their departure left Henry House understaffed and Lillian worked harder than ever. She led Red Cross drives. She made one of the settlement houses available to the draft board so boys could start their military career among friends. When the flu reached the epidemic stage, New York City officials grew panicky as relief and social agencies bogged down under the strain. They turned to Lillian, who had a genius for organization. With steadfast courage she united and mobilized organizational and lay workers, nurses to care for the sick, baby-sit, keep house, prepare and distribute soups, custards and linens to stricken families.

After the war, Lillian, having survived the gusts of ill-will with complete serenity, went full speed ahead with her plans for Henry House. Anxious to help legally employed children, she set up vocational courses at the settlement and offered vocational guidance. Whether a boy needed money, a job or the knowledge that someone believed in his abilities, she stood ready to help. For youngsters needing help to complete their education there was a scholarship committee that worked in cooperation with the public schools.

As the staff grew larger, Lillian found it hard to keep the informal friendly atmosphere she wanted. But somehow she managed a personal touch, making the group seem more like a family than an organization, a group that shared their victories, hopes, tragedies. Lillian's high degree of administrative ability, her sympathy, sincerity and charm attracted cooperation, loyalty and love.

The Henry Street settlement became famous. To the settlement came students of sociology, foreigners interested in setting up public health nursing in their own lands, social workers who wanted to study settlement techniques, celebrities, ordinary people who just wanted a look at this very special place or wanted to meet the generous and charming Lillian Wald.

Whenever possible, Lillian met guests at the door. Eminent visitors were welcome, but no more so than a man in frayed shirt sleeves or the woman who wrote, "My mother has told me you took care of me when I was born. Is it all right if I come to see you?"

Jane Addams of Hull House came to Henry Street. So did President Theodore Roosevelt, Supreme Court Justice Charles Evans Hughes, Prime Minister of England Ramsay MacDonald. When the famous Indian poet Rabindranath Tagore crossed the threshold in a long flowing gray robe, a little girl tugged at Lillian's hand and asked, "Is that God?"

All who came found the settlement an exciting place. With Lillian presiding at the dinner table the talk was sure to be spiced with wit and fun.

As the work of the settlement became widely known, Lillian received recognition—honorary degrees, awards, medals from Rotary Clubs and from the National Institute of Social Sciences for distinguished service to humanity.

As representative of the Federal Children's Bureau, she spoke at Cannes, France, at an International Red Cross Conference in 1919. Going on to Paris, Lillian met many of the distinguished men assembled to draft the Treaty of Versailles. As usual, she was always looking for some new idea or project she might take back to Henry Street.

Sadness came to Lillian when her mother, who had come to live with her on Henry Street, died in December 1923. "I am amazed," she wrote Uncle Samuel, "at the number of people who could have had no more than a fleeting impression of her who write of her beauty and loveliness."

The following spring Lillian accepted an invitation from the Russian government to visit the country and discuss public health measures. On the way she stopped in London to renew her acquaintance with Ramsay Mac-

Donald and other friends. From London she flew to Germany and then took a train to Moscow. The hustle and bustle surprised her; the sight of homeless children running around wild shocked her. Traveling from place to place Lillian found the plans for public health programs were in general sound, but clinics were badly kept, conditions at hospitals somewhat chaotic and nurses' training inadequate.

Back in New York September 9, Lillian resumed the old round of work eagerly, overtaxing herself to such an extent that her physician advised a vacation. Although Lillian protested, she finally consented to go to Mexico in the spring of 1925. With her went Jane Addams, who had become a dear friend.

In her letters Lillian had little to say about the way she was fêted by the president of Mexico and leading citizens. She did, however, write at length about "goats galore, huge wild poppies, mud-thatched huts, lemons on a stick and little boys in huge sombreros." Both Lillian and Jane were so engrossed in their settlements that they were always looking for experiences related to social work.

To recuperate from the surgery which became a necessity following the Mexican trip, Lillian went to the house she had bought on the banks of the Saugatuck near Westport, Connecticut, which she called House-on-the-Pond.

Her old self once more, Lillian took off for Italy in 1927, where she talked with Mussolini. Outwardly she found things better than on a previous trip. Trains were on time, beggars were fewer, but there was a lack of freedom. Before leaving Europe Lillian attended a session of the League of Nations in Geneva. Impressions of her trip abroad were written up in an article for *The Survey* magazine.

Home again Lillian buoyantly plunged into her work,

spearheading a drive to raise a half-million dollars for expansion of settlement activities. Having assembled proof that slums cost a tremendous sum in wrecked living and warped personalities, she tried to launch a campaign to rebuild the wretched, rat-infested, crumbling tenements of the East Side. But danger signs of oncoming depression made New Yorkers wary.

Although doctors warned her that she must slow up, and Lillian made fun of herself for her perpetual busyness, she couldn't seem to break the habit. Juggling her taxing jobs as administrator, fund-raiser, teacher, head of the settlement, supervisor of nurses, she still slept with a phone at her bedside to take care of emergencies, gave speeches, and served on committees with functions ranging from sanitation to preservation of civil liberties. Her organizational proficiency and initiative and the steel underneath her gentleness goaded committees to action.

The depression, which made Lillian's heart ache because it brought breadlines and more suffering to the East Side, further drained her energies. Unemployment of fathers meant less food and fuel, therefore more illness. To cope with the increasing number of calls for help, Lillian stepped up Henry House nursing activities. Much of her time was spent in conferences on unemployment, and relief committees. For East Siders she made up jobs and errands, discussed personal finances, expanded money services of the settlement.

Outwardly calm, patient, cheerful, Lillian was torn by social conditions around her and worked beyond her strength. She did finally yield to pleas of co-workers to attend fewer meetings and to spend a little more time at House-on-the-Pond. Lillian loved the flowers and trees, the tranquil house with large rooms, fireplaces and a screened porch. She reveled in looking at a sky unblocked by skyscrapers or in watching ducks waddling across the lawn. But while there she could never quite free herself from anxiety concerning what was going on in cold, drab tenements. Henry House was her real home. And the star she had followed so long, the star of service, still beckoned.

By 1932 Henry House was at the height of its activities, but also at the height of its need, Lillian thought ruefully, as starvation stalked the East Side and calls for help increased in frequency and insistency.

In January of the following year Lillian became very ill. Although she was in on the planning of the gala celebration of the fortieth anniversary of the founding of Henry House, she was too ill to attend the ceremonies. She was particularly pleased that presiding at the occasion was Joseph Levine, who had been a member of the Hero Club thirty-five years before.

A few weeks after the celebration, when it became clear to Lillian that she could never return to the complexity of the work at Henry House, she appointed Helen Hall, the brilliant, magnetic head of the University Settlement in Philadelphia, to succeed her. But she still retained the presidency and the staff continued to rely heavily on her level-headed judgment.

What Lillian Wald accomplished in her forty years at Henry House seems almost unbelievable, especially in view of the fact that she had no training in social work and had started out almost single-handed.

Today social workers usually prepare to enter only one of five areas—social casework, social group work, community organization, social administration, or social research. There are all kinds of specialists: child welfare, school caseworkers, psychiatric and medical social workers, teachers. To some extent Lillian served in all these categories.

A competent social worker is expected to have an undergraduate major in sociology, psychology, or economics, bulwarked by political science, history, anthropology, biology, English, plus graduate work in an approved school of social work. Lillian's experiences in nursing gave her some of this background, and she'd had an excellent cultural education, but any economics, sociology or psychology she knew was gained by self-education.

Through lectures, field trips, research, social workers today gain a workable knowledge of government procedures and laws, community organizations and resources. Lillian with her keen, flexible mind acquired all this information on the East Side, but through her own leg work and head work.

Schools of social work, when listing desirable traits for workers, enumerate a genuine interest in and respect for other people, objectivity, courage, tact, sense of humor, capacity to maintain friendly relations, integrity, imagination—especially an ability to see alternatives and find practical solutions. Lillian Wald possessed each of these to the fullest measure. Maturity, especially emotional maturity, cost her a good deal of self-discipline, but she did achieve it. She also had the requisites of good manners, neatness and, until in later years, good health.

Lillian respected the background of college-trained social workers who made application to join the Henry House staff, but she was more interested in their personalities than in the subjects they had studied. And she sometimes became impatient with the terminology and impersonal techniques of the professional social worker. Once when she asked a young college graduate to see a girl who needed some advice on child care, the graduate said nervously, "I haven't had any experience doing case work, I . . ."

"Who said anything about case work?" Lillian interrupted. "I asked you to go and see a girl."

Lillian's retreat to the House-on-the-Pond did not put a stop to her activities. Westport children loved her storytelling as much as the children on Henry Street. Crowds of them came to sit with her in the shade of a great elm or to play on her willow-hemmed pond. Adults came too—neighbors, friends, famous visitors like Jane Addams and Albert Einstein. They found her as warm and bright and gay as she had ever been. Mrs. Eleanor Roosevelt after a visit said, "I always fall under the spell of her personality. To know her is to love her." Even when confined to her bed, Lillian kept in touch with all that went on at Henry House and in the world around her, and the world kept touch with her. There were dozens of telephone calls, and each letter in the stacks of mail that came to her was answered personally. Still not resigned to giving up the stir and clamor of Henry Street, Lillian pushed her thoughts ahead to new projects.

On February 12, 1936, Lillian was chosen by students of the Abraham Lincoln High School in Brooklyn to receive the Lincoln Medallion awarded to the citizen rendering greatest service to the city of New York.

Lillian's birthdays had always been gala occasions on Henry Street. Friends, settlement workers, old club members, firemen, policemen had always decorated, hammered, costumed and staged elaborate pageants. Unable to attend the celebration of her seventieth birthday, March 10, 1937, Lillian listened to the proceedings in her honor via radio. Review of her accomplishments may have been lacking in oratory, but the deep sincerity of the participants was readily apparent. Although appreciative of the tributes, Lillian kept insisting that credit be given to those who had been her co-workers—people like Mary Brewster, Florence Kelley, Lavinia Dock. There was an avalanche of birthday cards, telegrams, gifts, fruits, flowers. Letters came from all over the world—letters written in childish scrawls, letters from scrubwomen, East Siders, immigrants, factory workers and factory owners, writers, artists, Mayor La Guardia of New York, and the President of the United States.

A group of Westport children presented her with flowers and a huge scrapbook in which writers had contributed bits of verse, artists had drawn sketches. In the book twelve hundred people had signed their names—some in childish scrawl, others in the unsteady letters of the aged. Each had contributed to a fund for Henry Street.

That same year a large New York playground was named for Lillian D. Wald, "In appreciation of her pioneer work for children and district nursing in this city."

Even when Lillian's illness became more confining, her joyousness bubbled over. If she couldn't live out of bed she would live in it. She bantered with her nurse and secretary. Visitors still saw a woman with an air of composure and authority, who had a kindly concern for everyone. From a bed strewn with letters, books, telegrams, clippings, Lillian wrote her second book, *Windows on Henry Street,* based on her own experiences on the East Side. It also included some of her pet theories concerning the welfare of children. Aroused by the thunder of dictatorships abroad and the mushrooming of bigotry, she wrote articles on brotherhood.

In 1939 Lillian retired officially, handing the presidency

of Henry House over to John M. Schiff, grandson of the Jacob H. Schiff who had done so much to help the settlement get started.

The following year the number of days when visitors were banned increased. But Lillian's steady radiance of spirit and temper remained undimmed. She died September 1, 1940.

The eulogies were many. But the sad faces of children, policemen, scrubwomen and businessmen on Henry Street told who would miss her the most. From thousands of East Siders who had known Lillian Wald as the Angel of Henry Street there was a full-throated farewell.

Lillian Wald didn't *talk* about feeling sorry for or loving the baffled, underprivileged, unfortunate; she loved them. With faith, courage and disregard for self, she tenaciously fulfilled her goals, never in the spirit of a martyr but with unfailing good humor. Imaginative, she worked with people the way an artist works with colors.

Like ripples spreading over a pond Lillian Wald's work goes on. All over New York there are reminders of her influence—Henry House, playgrounds, the housing project named for her after her death. Many of New York's leading citizens got their start because of opportunities offered at Henry House. Lillian Wald helped give New Yorkers a social conscience. Today, because of her work, the East Side is a better place to live in. And then there are the visiting nurses. Their importance has been recognized by many universities with faculties devoted to public health nursing. Students, in addition to nurse's training, get special instruction in the handling of statistics, in community responsibilities and the relationship of patients to their environment. There are thousands of public health nurses in the employ of municipal, county, state and federal agencies. Throughout the world, visiting nurses work in cities, but they also travel lonely mountain trails with pioneer resourcefulness and courage. There are never enough visiting nurses or social workers to fill job openings.

Lillian Wald's life is a challenge to all who would serve. In places made dark by hunger, illness, injustice, the Angel of Henry Street saw what needed to be done and did it. She gave an unwavering love of humanity and got it in return—that was what she believed in.

## 3: AGNES DE MILLE

### Rebel in Ballet Slippers

A ballerina's aerial jumps, pirouettes, and flowing gestures give the impression of simplicity and lack of effort. But it takes years of training, persistence and discipline to acquire the techniques of a mature dancer and to train the body to the point where it can be trusted. Fourteen years elapsed between Agnes de Mille's arrival in New York as an unknown and her starred appearances in *Rodeo*—failure-studded years of grueling work and relentless concentration on dancing.

Remarkably tenacious in her experimentation with gestures and rhythms, Agnes pioneered in American ballet, becoming the first woman to distinguish herself in choreography. To many people who had never cared for the old classical forms, she made ballet understandable.

Agnes was born in New York City. Her father was a playwright, her mother the daughter of the famous economist, Henry George. At an early age Agnes dreamed of being an actress in her father's plays, but the dream faded after she saw Danish-born ballerina Adeline Génée give an exquisite performance. "I want to take ballet lessons," she announced after the concert. Mrs. de Mille, who feared rigid ballet training would interfere with Agnes' self-expression, refused to arrange for lessons.

When Mr. de Mille's show *After Five* folded, Agnes'

movie producer Uncle Cecil urged him to try Hollywood, and the family went West. Agnes was disillusioned when she found that in Hollywood the only Indians and most of the cowboys were those on movie sets.

With Margaret she attended the Hollywood School for Girls, where classes were held outdoors in good weather. Alert and intelligent, Agnes breezed through her class work. Her favorite subject was pantomime. Sometimes the loyalty of the de Mille girls to their Uncle Cecil's Paramount Pictures erupted in squabbles with daughters of rival producers.

In out-of-school hours Agnes had dozens of projects and magic secret games. For her dolls she made whole wardrobes of clothes. She also liked to paint in exact colors the wildflowers she found in the woods, where violets were not just flowers but breath-taking surprises. Possessed of a lively imagination, Agnes directed her sister Margaret and their playmates in dance pageants under the banana tree and in melodramas, or bossed them in the building of everything from an inn with thatched roof and brick floor to a palace built of boxes, crates and sawed-off palm branches. Astride the ridge pole of the castle, which Agnes describes as being "ten feet above reality," she enjoyed golden moments that compensated for such irksome routines as going to bed early or having to wear rubbers. Plans for completely furnishing the palace were terminated abruptly when Mrs. de Mille found that Agnes and her friends had been raiding dumps on their way home from school. A bundle of false swords Uncle Cecil gave her after the movie *Joan of Arc* helped offset this disappointment. At games like tag Agnes was active and agile—none could ever catch her.

Mrs. de Mille, who had very definite ideas on the rear-ing of children, held the girls to high intellectual and moral standards. In some respects she was almost stern. Despite their father's very adequate income, the girls had small allowances. They were not permitted to read newspapers, and in high school they dined alone and went to bed at nine o'clock. Wanting the girls to look like ladies, Mrs. de Mille required them to wear scarves, shade hats and gloves to keep them from becoming sun-tanned. Mrs. de Mille expected her girls to be gentle and sweet, but also competent and well-informed. Each morning while her mother combed Agnes' thick, red-gold hair, Agnes read aloud in French, although Mrs. de Mille did not understand the language. Mrs. de Mille's father had been a genius; she took it for granted that with proper training her daughters would also be outstanding. Under the penetrating scrutiny of her mother's blue eyes, Agnes learned by the time she was ten to discuss intelligently such terms as initiative and referendum.

On rare occasions and under proper chaperonage, Agnes and Margaret were permitted to visit their Uncle Cecil's studio—a converted stable on Vine Street. Agnes found the open-air stages under the feathery pepper trees places of enchantment. She saw Gloria Swanson fed to the lions and Geraldine Farrar burned at the stake.

On holidays Agnes and Margaret often went to Uncle Cecil's house. Despite flower-filled rooms, library and luxurious swimming pool, the atmosphere was homey and family talk was as enjoyable as the unusual entertainment Uncle Cecil sometimes provided. At Christmas time he gave the girls expensive, grown-up gifts such as French perfume.

Oftener than they liked, Agnes and Margaret were called upon to share in one of their mother's public appearances when she spoke at civic occasions or laid a wreath on a public monument. The sisters were proud of her accomplishments, but often grew restless waiting for the end of the ceremonies.

Many of Agnes' activities were dictated by her father whom she adored, and who was well-versed not only in show business, but in art, music, literature and photography. If her father recommended a certain book, Agnes felt impelled to read it. Hope of being able to accompany her father, who was an accomplished singer, spurred her into piano practice. Because her father was an amateur photographer, Agnes went in for picture taking. Because he played tennis unusually well, she played tennis. Her energetic game repeatedly won her a berth as a semifinalist in the California Junior State Tournament.

Life in the de Mille household was never dull. Artists, writers, lecturers, movie producers, clubwomen, musicians and scientists came in droves to the large house flanked by a garden fragrant with lavender, amaryllis, narcissus, and primroses. There were actors and actresses too, although they came less frequently since Mr. de Mille thought he saw enough of show people in his work. Agnes admired the grace and poise of the dazzling women and enjoyed the actors like Charlie Chaplin, who did incredible imitations. To all who came Mrs. de Mille dispensed tea, kindness and economic theories.

Agnes' glamorous experiences with celebrities somewhat compensated for lack of the ballet lessons she craved. But one day she saw the great Russian ballerina, Anna Pavlova. The flashing grace, yet steely vitality of the radiant-faced dancer made Agnes drift off into a world quite unlike the everyday one of lessons, packing-box castles and childish arguments. As she left the theater her head pounded and she could hardly swallow. Once more Agnes asked longingly for ballet lessons, but her parents vetoed the suggestion.

Denied lessons, Agnes read every book on ballet she could get hold of. She made a scrapbook of pictures of dancers. She began improvising routines of her own. When she heard the famous dancer Isadora Duncan advise running barefoot over the hills, Agnes tried it, ending up with cactus spines in her feet.

Finally Agnes' chance came in an unexpected way. Margaret began suffering from fallen arches. An orthopedist recommended ballet lessons to strengthen her feet. What one sister did, the other always shared.

The day the sisters enrolled at the Kosloff School of Imperial Russian Ballet, Agnes' muscles felt knotted by excitement. Here was her chance; she'd make the most of it, she promised herself as they entered a large bare room with white walls that smelled of soap, perspiring dancers and the hot glue in overworked ballet slippers. On three sides of the room was a rail that Agnes knew was a *barre* used for steadying one's self while exercising. At the end of the room there was a large mirror.

Agnes' audition with the slender, supple Kosloff, an ex-member of Diaghilev's Ballets Russes, was disappointing. He criticized her weight, her stance, her weak knees. "Thirteen is a little old to start training," he told her.

Nevertheless, Agnes was accepted. She was to have one class lesson and one private lesson a week. Class lessons were stimulating but exhausting. Agnes had no idea there would be so many hours of stretching the spine or arranging her feet in fixed positions before one got to do jumps and spins. With aching back, calves and shoulders she would look in the mirror at her short legs and arms, her overweight body, and envy the tall, slender girls who could more easily achieve graceful, classic lines. Sometimes Kosloff stamped, beat time with a cane, roared and denounced laggards, making the lesson a frightening experience. Handicapped by the fact that she usually missed warming-up exercises because a piano lesson scheduled just ahead of dancing class almost always made her late, Agnes started cold. Feeling herself the worst pupil in her class, she was excited on the one day when Kosloff called upon her to demonstrate to the class an exercise in pantomime. Twice Agnes fainted in class, but got little sympathy.

The private lessons she loved, although the dark-haired Miss Fredova, thin as a sapling, was a strict disciplinarian. Gradually Agnes learned the basic postures, arabesques and pirouettes. She also learned that even when her lungs felt like bursting she must give her hands and body the appearance of floating. When her head became feverish she cooled it by leaning against the plastered wall —no student was permitted to sit down.

Because Miss Fredova, who was both patient and kind, instilled in her the necessity of work, of discipline, of devotion, she never missed a daily practice. Agnes' progress was not spectacular, but her stocky, sturdy body gained in endurance, her coordination improved, her legs strengthened and she became a good jumper. Three times during the winter Miss Fredova regarded her with a, "Very good." These instances Agnes duly recorded in her diary.

Despite the hard work and discipline, Agnes loved dancing and begged for more lessons, pointing out that most of the ballet students practically lived at the studio.

"You can practice at home," her parents told her.

Lacking the supervision the others had, Agnes developed rigid bad habits. Conscious of her lack of progresss compared with the rest of the pupils, she crept around at the rear of the group during class lessons, finding excuses to retie her shoes—any activity aside from dancing. Many nights she cried herself to sleep.

Partly because of her frustration over not being allowed to spend more time at the Kosloff Studio, Agnes plunged into a welter of activities. In addition to ballet exercises she practiced piano for two hours daily and groomed the family's seven fox terriers. She was editor of the school paper, captain of the tennis team.

"You have to drop something," Mrs. de Mille told her. Agnes gathered that the something was preferably dancing.

Then Agnes saw Pavlova again. Rapturously she watched the nimble, airy-footed ballerina go through her paces with effortless perfection. But what affected her most was Pavlova's sincerity and absorption in beauty. To Agnes it seemed as if through her dancing one caught a glimpse of something divine. That was what Agnes wanted to do in her own dancing.

After the performance Agnes filed backstage to meet the ballerina. When Pavlova kissed her and gave her a handful of carnations and cherry blossoms, Agnes almost burst with joy and pride. She felt as if her whole life had been altered. Now truly she had a vision, a goal.

Dancing became a madness with Agnes. It was flight and freedom. Unless she could dance like Pavlova her whole life would be without meaning. Agnes' mind was so full of fantasies about receiving praise from Pavlova that they kept getting mixed in with her Latin verbs or her a plus b equals x, although she still maintained a straight A average.

But when she gave signs of making a career of dancing her parents discouraged her. There was nothing to indicate that she was an unusually gifted dancer, Mrs. de Mille argued. Her father objected to having a daughter of his give her life to acrobatics. Agnes had been brought up to be a lady, and ladies didn't dance. Anyway ballet required unflagging effort—the work was hard, the reward small.

But Agnes, who had a one-track mind, didn't intend to be talked out of a career in ballet. It was hard, though, to keep her singleness of purpose in the face of parental opposition, and it hurt when her father took no interest in what went on at the Kosloff School even when students gave performances.

Mrs. de Mille tried to get Agnes' mind off ballet by involving her in social activities, but met with little success. When boys came to the house Agnes was likely to challenge them to a game of tennis. After a thorough drubbing they didn't come back. Trying another tack, Mrs. de Mille sent Agnes off to junior cotillions with her hair piled high on top of her head and topped by a laurel wreath which Agnes detested. She was a poor social dancer, too intellectual a conversationalist. Sitting out most of the dances, she comforted herself with the thought that one of these days she'd be a great ballerina. She was a little wistful about her sister Margaret's suitors, her flowers and long telephone conversations, but ballet seemed more important.

As time went on, Agnes' prospects for a dancing career got bleaker and bleaker. In class she seemed to be making no progress at all. Dancing meant exhaustion and little else. Because of tides of people and lack of privacy, practicing at home became increasingly difficult. To the garden parties, teas, shows or evenings of music came celebrities Mrs. de Mille wanted Agnes to meet or help entertain—Somerset Maugham, Rebecca West, the Zimbalists.

With such interesting people around, going off to practice seemed lonely and distasteful.

Upon graduation from high school Agnes was confronted with the necessity of choosing between dancing and a college education. Maybe there were too many factors against her, she reasoned, to have a future in ballet—her build, the late start, her restricted lessons. And she couldn't bear to go counter to the ardent desire of her parents who wanted her to go on to college and become a writer.

So Agnes entered the University of California. She enjoyed the new freedom of reading newspapers, putting up her own hair, eating what she wanted for lunch. Never a person to make a half-hearted approach to living, she concentrated furiously on her English major and related subjects, by-passing football games, parties, dancing—both social and ballet. Although she was studying almost to the point of dropping, Agnes wheedled the dean into letting her take extra hours.

After Agnes joined Kappa Alpha Theta sorority she dated occasionally and became involved in some of the social affairs of the campus. In order to condition herself to dance at a benefit for student victims of a campus fire, she resumed her daily ballet routines. Later a South Sea Island number done to the accompaniment of tom-toms was very favorably received at a student assembly. Almost before she realized it, Agnes was back on a schedule of familiar dance routines. When her father encountered her dancing in an upstairs hallway he snorted, "All this education and I'm still the father of a circus."

One Sunday afternoon Agnes was practicing in the living room. She was startled when she looked up and saw her sister Margaret with the talented seventeen-year-old

[73]

actor Douglass Montgomery. "You're no amateur," Douglass said to Agnes. "You're a great performer."

Agnes and Douglass became good friends. Both had one-track minds, both were passionately ambitious, both loved to talk about the theater. Dug implored Agnes to get out from under parental domination and go to New York for training.

A week-long engagement which Dug arranged for Agnes at the Pasadena Playhouse made up her mind for her. She was going to be a dancer. But the road ahead seemed beset by obstacles. She was already nineteen; her body was heavy and flabby, her vitality low; her mechanics still had to be perfected; her parents had to be convinced. Mr. de Mille yielded more readily than Agnes had expected. But he did want her to finish her college education since she was so close to a degree. She graduated *magna cum laude,* but the honor meant very little to her. She would have preferred to be dancing in *Les Sylphides.*

The day after graduation, Agnes' parents told her they were getting a divorce. Agnes was stunned. To comfort her mother she accompanied her on a summer-long tour of Europe. For the most part they sat around in *pensions;* there were no theaters, no dancing. Agnes was restless and melancholy.

Upon their return Agnes decided to live in New York with her mother, but she missed her father's vital and stimulating personality. The allowance Mr. de Mille sent would have been ample for simple living, but Agnes' mother was determined to live in her accustomed style. Agnes chafed under her mother's supervision, but she didn't like the prospect of abandoning a lonely woman.

The routines at the ballet school Agnes chose were haphazard and inefficient compared to the Kosloff Studio. But she practiced faithfully and began giving auditions to agents. Agnes had never before hunted work. There was still a lot of toughness and vulgarity in the show business in the 1920's; and the ladylike, well-educated Agnes, who used meticulous English, impressed agents as being a snob. Anyway, they were looking mostly for dancers skilled in tap or line routines. Ballet, unless strictly comedy, left them disinterested or lukewarm. The word choreography was unknown.

Dug, who had come from Hollywood to play in *God Loves Us,* still held high hopes for Agnes. "But do something about your clothes," he begged. "What you need is to build your commercial appeal." For building that appeal Dug had various suggestions ranging from dyeing her hair to changing her name—he didn't think the name Agnes would look well in front of a theater.

Agnes did not resort to any such superficial measures, but she and Dug did work a great deal together. He taught her how to establish mood with a posture, how to give gestures a more explicit meaning. Heartened by Dug's praise, Agnes began working hopefully toward the goal of private recitals. With no concert date, no fixed schedule, no real coach, Agnes found it difficult to discipline herself, but she practiced doggedly.

Finally through Mrs. de Mille's writer friend, Mary Austin, a recital was arranged for in Santa Fe. Arriving at the theater for the rehearsal, Agnes found the floor too splintery for dancing. Mrs. de Mille, a resourceful and energetic woman, got a man with a planing machine to smooth the boards, and she personally puttied the cracks.

The intensity of the heat in the theater, which was not air-conditioned, made Agnes feel as if suffocation might overtake her at any moment. And she was disconcerted by the presence of a number of Indians in the audience who thought her dancing was hilarious. Despite these drawbacks, the recital was fairly successful. "Say your prayers and you will be a good dancer," Mary Austin told Agnes later. "And don't feel sorry for yourself."

Back in New York, Agnes had several short engagements which led to scheduling a recital to be shared with Jacques Cartier. Telephone calls, flowers, a telegram from Mr. de Mille before the concert gave Agnes the feeling of having arrived. The audience applause was enormous, but Agnes was disturbed by their reactions. Her goal had been to give audiences beauty, to carry them into sublime moods as Pavlova had done. Yet dances she considered to be full of pathos and tragedy drew laughter. She was even more distressed when newspapers next day hailed her as a comedienne.

Thinking that the failure to convey the beauty she wanted to give must lie in her lack of technique, Agnes worked to develop smoothness that would make spectators unaware of the mechanics of her dancing. She gave more auditions for cigar-smoking agents, who customarily kept their hats and coats on during the try-outs. For a while Agnes' sense of humor buoyed her up. But she began to be a little panicky—nothing seemed to lead to worthwhile engagements. And when after an audition Noel Coward, who was attentive and courteous, told her she belonged in a concert hall, not the theater, Agnes' expectations plummeted almost to the zero point. It began to dawn on her that no matter how beautifully she danced there wouldn't be a place for her in the theater. Most people just didn't appreciate the Pavlova type of dancing.

In the autumn of 1928 Adolph Bohm invited her to be soloist on a tour to cities as scattered as Pittsburgh, Chicago, Des Moines, Macon. The tarnished shabbiness of the troupe of ill-assorted, second-rate dancers depressed Agnes, and some of the roughhousing shocked her Victorian sensibilities. The fatherly and kind orchestral conductor, Louis Horst, often gave her advice and reassurances, taught her some of the basic techniques of being a good trouper and helped her find decent hotels and places to eat.

As the routines of intricate steps became habitual for Agnes, she grew more and more interested in choreography. She found it challenging to fit together music, dance steps, facial expressions and gestures so they would tell a story. Agnes got the opportunity to try out some of her own ideas when she was engaged to do the choreography for and to dance *The Black Crook*. Her dancing partner was pugnacious but idealistic Warren Leonard. He didn't like the way she dressed and mercilessly criticized her slowness, weight and timidity. He objected to Mrs. de Mille's interference. A believer in a routine of no food, no rest, no conversation during rehearsals, he often reduced Agnes to the point of exhaustion. But her technique improved.

*The Black Crook* gave Agnes a very trying three months. During one performance Warren accidentally kicked her in the nose and broke it. She had to finish the week with splints up her nose. When spring came, late-night-showgoers bombarded the dancers with peanuts, popcorn, beer coasters, midst catcalls and drunken singing. Agnes quit the show. Because she had splurged on costumes she had no money left for decent street clothes.

After several other engagements which were unsuccesssful financially and seemed to be leading nowhere, Agnes and Mrs. de Mille returned to Hollywood. Wanting to maintain an ascetic seclusion, they stayed at a hotel instead

[77]

of with relatives. A successful recital at the Music Box Theater was followed by banner headlines; DE MILLE GIRL MAKES GOOD. Whereupon Uncle Cecil offered to road-show Agnes through the United States. But Agnes couldn't see any future for her dancing in the kind of extravaganza he had in mind. She wanted her dancing to be so meaningful that she wouldn't have to rely on scenery, lush orchestration or supporting dancers. When she made a counter-proposal—a chance in the movies, Uncle Cecil told her he couldn't hire anyone who was related to him, and anyway she was non-photogenic.

For a while Agnes lived with her father, who had married Clara Beranger. Although Mr. de Mille listened sympathetically to Agnes' plans for private recitals, he was in deep water financially because of the depression and felt he couldn't invest in her. Backing or no backing, Agnes was determined to go on dancing.

When she told her mother she planned to return to New York but was going to find a place of her own, which would insure the freedom she needed for rehearsing, Mrs. de Mille wept and protested. But she eventually became reconciled, and went along, on Agnes' terms.

The rooms Agnes rented in a third-rate hotel were so dark that she could hardly tell noon from midnight, but at least she could do just as she pleased. Agnes settled down to learn choreography. She experimented to find new movements to symbolize emotions, rather than use standard ballet gestures such as touching the lips with the fingers to symbolize a kiss. It occurred to her that good portraits reveal that which is within, and in a sense every gesture is a portrait.

Seeking to develop a form of dance that would be more understandable to theater-goers than the old classic ballets such as *Swan Lake,* Agnes became interested in American folk dances, which she found wild and exciting. But for the kind of thing she wanted to do—making ballet deal with situations and emotions of daily life instead of with children's dream fantasies—there was no pattern to follow. To get the movements, she had to dance them. In her experimentation she drew heavily on her musical and literary knowledge and also studied scenery, design, lighting.

Except for the dancer, Martha Graham, no one seemed to understand what Agnes was trying to do—least of all theatrical agents. Although Mrs. de Mille neither approved nor understood, she continued to turn out costumes with ruffles, rosettes and embroidery; ran errands; sold most of her bonds to pay recital expenses, then badgered people into attending them. All the while she kept believing in Agnes' ultimate success.

Agnes seized every opportunity that came her way, even minor appearances at third-rate movies and night clubs. Finally, she got the chance to do the dances for *Flying Colors,* but from the first everything seemed to go wrong. The dancers were incompetent and indifferent to Agnes' perfectionism. There were miscalculations in scenery and costumes.

Under the stress of a deadline and of bickering and tension, Agnes' creativity went dead. Another choreographer was called in.

Things got progressively worse. With America in the grip of a depression, the openings in show business dwindled, and Agnes didn't have funds to finance private recitals, which then cost in the neighborhood of twelve hundred dollars. "Better forget dancing," her friends advised. "Why all this experimentation anyway?"

A person with less stick-to-itiveness would have folded,

[79]

but not Agnes. Dancing was more important to her than anything else. It wasn't that fame or fortune beckoned; it was just that within her was this creative urge for expres‑ sion. Somehow she had to find a way to popularize ballet without sacrificing artistic qualities.

But at times when no recital was in sight and Agnes' own dance routines seemed to be going stale, she would become lonely, baffled and discouraged. Then she would seek out her friend Martha Graham. Although the famous dancer refused to take Agnes as a student, her criticism was invaluable. "We all go through periods like this," she would assure Agnes. "There is achievement ahead."

One day after Martha had told her rather sternly that she "must find her own way," Agnes asked, "But, practi‑ cally, Martha, what do I do?"

"Make yourself a program of activity," she advised. "Do not stop once for five minutes to consider what you are doing. Keep going."

It was Martha Graham who made Agnes see that she had a unique gift and that she would be blocked in her expression of it if she thought only of self or of mechanics. "Of you I expect something more than technique," Martha scolded.

By now Mrs. de Mille's funds were very limited, but Agnes and she decided that they could swing a series of recitals by going to Europe where expenses would be only about a fifth as great.

Because of poor publicity, Agnes got a frosty welcome at her Parisian debut. There was not one bit of applause when she appeared on stage. During the first dance she slipped and fell on the new linoleum floor covering. But she went on to dance brilliantly and to win repeated cur‑ tain calls. Later she discovered her manager had **disap‑ peared,** taking the gate receipts with him.

Agnes danced in Brussels and then London, where she won the attention of the critics who appreciated her spontaneous, yet controlled dancing. She began at least to break even on her recitals.

When she decided to stay in England and study with Madame Marie Rambert, who had a reputation for developing techniques and correctness of step, Mrs. de Mille returned to America.

Shrieking denunciations, Madame Rambert, a small woman with jet black hair and smoldering eyes, put Agnes and other students through their paces in a big, damp, chilly room always filled with a grayish light. "Long your arms," Madame would say to Agnes, pulling them until Agnes felt they were being removed from their sockets. But her movements became more precise, eloquent, and truthful. As her skill was perfected, her honest striving toward "something greater than technique" that Martha Graham had talked about began to show in originality and power, earning warm-hearted encouragement from Madame Rambert.

Agnes' continuing interest in popularizing ballet through combining folk dances with ballet techniques led her into intensive study, research, experimentation. Much of her practicing was carried out with Antony Tudor and Hugh Laing—both Rambert students. Antony, who had a gigantic talent, was gentle, courteous, quiet. A tiger on bad days, Hugh could be very good company on his better days. The trio frequently took time off from their dancing to talk, walk, share midnight suppers, explore the docks and fascinating places in town and countryside. Agnes also met people prominent in social and literary circles—Lady Asquith, Barnard Shaw.

Critics cheered Agnes' recitals and her choreography in *Nymph Errant*. At a charity bazaar she danced before the

Prince of Wales. But living in a shilling-in-the-meter attic was bleak, and the arduous dancing combined with details of finance, management, publicity left Agnes exhausted.

Packing her tarlatans, ballet slippers, wigs and press notices, she headed for home. In New York, she mailed notices, visited agents, practiced relentlessly. But by the time she had paid studio rent, wages to supporting dancers and accompanists, bought costumes and met the expenses of publicity, she was in the red again.

Hurok's importation of the Ballet Russe in 1935 made competition even tougher. Once more Agnes went West. She hired a cast of eighty dancers for a Hollywood Bowl performance. The dancing was good, but the lighting effects made it impossible to tell a man from a woman or blue from red. Agnes lost a thousand dollars, and one newspaper came out with caption: DE MILLE GIRL FAILS.

Agnes was offered a chance for some choreography in the movie *Romeo and Juliet*, but difficulties developed when the filming began. Parts of dances she held dear were cut out or ruined by faulty lighting or wrong camera angles. When it became clear she'd either have to sacrifice her idealism about dancing or quit the movies, Agnes resigned.

After another unsuccessful venture or two, Agnes returned to London. Here she prepared extensively for private recitals. Several of her studies, including some American dances that later formed the nucleus for *Rodeo,* were well received. With twelve girls she worked out a series of concerts that critics acclaimed, but the company broke up for lack of money. And it was September, 1939. England was preparing for war, aliens were being sent home—Agnes was among them.

In New York Mrs. de Mille had rented a cheerful and

convenient studio for Agnes. She launched upon a period of Spartan-like living and of stock-taking. She was healthy, hard-working, dedicated—why was she failing? Part of her trouble, she knew, lay in the undue control exercised by two or three critics, part in the popular belief that had grown since importation of the Ballet Russe, that only Russians could do ballet. The Ballet Russe de Monte, direct descendant of the original Diaghilev Ballet, was nearly all European—mostly Russian. If, as occasionally happened, Americans had such outstanding talent as to be accepted into the company, they were asked to Russianize their names.

But what about herself, Agnes wanted to know, was holding her back? She began to pay more attention to clothes and personal grooming and she resolved to be more punctual and better organized. The thing she had to do, she realized, was to release the unique gift that was hers—it might not be great, but it was different from anyone else's, and it was up to her to develop it.

The Ballet Theater, founded in 1940, gave Agnes her first chance at choreography, in *Black Ritual*. Afterwards, Louis Pryor booked her for a national tour. She used it as an opportunity to work out some of her ideas on a distinctly American type of ballet. Ordinary people, the people she had dreamed of reaching, liked her work. Almost as soon as she was back in New York she did the choreography for and danced the lead in *Three Virgins and a Devil*. Agnes enjoyed doing it and it pleased the critics.

But by now America was convulsed by World War II. Agnes assumed that concert work was over for the duration. Feeling she had had her chance and muffed it, she decided she'd better join the w.a.c. or get a job. About this time she met Walter Foy Prude. A few days after their

first tea he was drafted, but Agnes and he kept up a correspondence.

When Agnes got wind that the Ballet Russe de Monte
Carlo, which now included some non-Russians, was considering a new work, possibly an American ballet, Agnes
submitted *Rodeo,* which she had started working on in
London. *Rodeo* is a love story with the American South-
west for its setting. It centers around a tomboyish Cowgirl
who, with the odds against her, sets out to get a man.
When her desperate efforts seem to be failing, she is miserable and concludes that she is no good as a woman or
a cowhand. But in the end she wins the Champion Roper.
There is a good deal of riding, roping and square dancing
set to the sometimes rowdy, but always rhythmic, melodies
of Aaron Copland.

The director complained that it was like putting a mustache on a Rembrandt painting to have the classically
trained ballet members impersonating cowboys. But when
the Russians entrained for the West on a tour with another
ballet, Agnes was along to get rehearsals started for the
forthcoming *Rodeo.*

It was hard for Agnes to make her ideas understandable,
especially to those in the company who spoke only Russian. When the men stopped moving like wind-blown
petals and began walking like cowboys squinting against
an imaginary sun, Agnes knew she'd gotten across to
them.

Between rehearsals Agnes spent interminable days on
hot, stuffy, untidy railroad coaches. On stopovers the stars
of the Ballet Russe lived in first-class hotels, but Agnes
stayed at dingy ones eating sandwiches or malted milks
with the cast at dinner time, and dinner at midnight. In
off-hours, using a combination of Russian and English,
Agnes chatted with the travel-weary, underpaid girls as

they sat around mending their tights or sewing ribbons on slippers worn out at the rate of a pair a week.

On October 16, 1942, the golden curtains in the Metropolitan Opera House parted for the opening of *Rodeo*. Squinting out from under a cowgirl hat, Agnes danced the lead in a state of semiconsciousness, although she was alert enough to know that much was wrong. Some of the lines were crooked; a few of the girls clapped off beat. Agnes' collar was so tight she almost fainted. As the heavy curtains closed she sneezed because of the dust from the lining, and thought, I've made so many foolish mistakes.

But the audience was less critical. Touched by the tenderness, the humor, the pithy portrayal of cowboy character, they gave the cast a rousing ovation. When her dancing partner Frederic Franklin gently pushed Agnes forward, she was presented with a large bunch of corn tied with red, white and blue ribbons. Then followed armloads of flowers. There were twenty-two curtain calls.

To Broadway, Agnes' success was a surprise, but not to people who knew of the years of hard work.

"Aren't you proud of her?" some friends asked Mrs. de Mille.

"I've always been proud of her," Mrs. de Mille answered. "Always. When no one hired her."

The hour Agnes de Mille had prepared for for fourteen years had finally struck. She called Walter at the Aberdeen Proving Grounds. "I knew it would be a success," he told her.

Spectacular offers poured in. Most of them Agnes bypassed to keep herself free to join Walter when leaves came his way.

But she couldn't resist dancing at the Philharmonic Auditorium in Los Angeles. It was there that she had seen Pavlova and the dream of becoming a great dancer had stirred within her. Agnes danced her own work with a virtuoso partner, Freddie Franklin, to an auditorium packed with friends, movie producers, talent scouts and little girls who watched as intensely as she had once watched Pavlova. At the end of the recital the hall echoed with cries of "Bravo! Agnes de Mille!" Her dedication had paid off. With her arms full of carnations and roses, Agnes walked off-stage to find her father waiting for her.

"You have come a long way," he told her.

When Agnes was asked to do the choreography for *Oklahoma!* she decided she would make no attempt to present a lavish spectacle, but rely on human interest and true American style. She would use every dance to heighten character and mood, and the ballet to advance the plot. Fierce and intense in her perfectionism, she fretted about the dances all through rehearsals.

The night the show opened the audience caught the honesty, gaiety, and Americanism of the show. They laughed, they applauded and went home singing:

> Oh, what a beautiful mornin'
> Oh, what a beautiful day.

But Agnes was dissatisfied. She stubbornly insisted on reorganizing the play and staging new numbers. Everyone pitched in to help. When sickness caught up with some of the cast, others filled in for the absentees. Agnes herself had to take time out for German measles.

The revised show was a smash hit. In fact, it was phe- nomenal, starting a new trend on Broadway. In terms of box-office receipts and applause it broke every record. Immediately Agnes received offers from Paramount and M.G.M. Agents, reporters, musicians, dancers wanted urgently to talk to her.

Success did not change Agnes de Mille. Her dedication to ballet kept pushing her toward a greater perfection. And Martha Graham kept insisting Agnes had not fulfilled her possibilities. "There is a vitality, a life force translated through you into action," Martha said, "Your business is to keep the channel open."

After *Oklahoma!* success followed success—*One Touch of Venus, Bloomer Girl, Carousel, Brigadoon.* Most of Agnes' work was dappled with humor, but not the *The Harvest According,* with a Civil War setting and men departing for war, or *Fall River Legend.* The latter was a melodrama founded on fact. In the summer of 1892 a respectable spinster by the name of Lizzie Borden was accused of hacking her father and stepmother to death with an ax, but was finally acquitted. Despite the fact that one critic referred to it as a "whodunit on toes," Agnes' adroit handling made *Fall River Legend* a hit.

In 1943 Agnes married Walter Prude. They spent their honeymoon in routine wartime fashion, cooped up in a small house with four other Army families. For ten hectic weeks Agnes put in long, lonely hours waiting for brief meetings with Walter. Then he was sent overseas. After his departure no news came at all. Agnes was tense, worried, snappish. She slept little and often awakened in a nightmare of fear. She wasn't pretty, and no housekeeper at all. Would Walter still love her when he got back?

As soon as Agnes knew where Walter was, she sent long letters and small gifts and planned how things would be when this strange period of death in life should end. At a studio in Greenwich Village she tried to continue her work.

After the war Agnes and Walter took a small apartment in New York. A son, Jonathan, was born in 1946.

Temporarily Agnes abandoned Broadway, but she

didn't give up dancing or thinking about it. The honors and awards which had started coming her way in 1943 with the New York Critics' and Donaldson Award kept right on. In 1946 she was chosen "Woman of the Year" by the New York Press Women. She received the Lord and Taylor award in 1947; also the Antoinette Perry Award, and in 1953 the Alumni Award of the University of California. She has been honored by Lit.D., *Honoris Causa* from Mills College, Russell Sage College, Smith College, and Western College for Women.

For some time Agnes had jotted down memos and impressions on letter paper, wrapping paper, envelopes, programs whenever she had moments to spare—on buses, subways, in doctors' waiting rooms. These had accumulated in dresser drawers and hatboxes. Gradually she pulled them together. The result was *Dance to the Piper*, an autobiographical book which proved that her father's faith in her literary ability had been justified. Her keen observations and acute sense of humor enliven the account of her long struggle to become a dancer.

In this book and also in an article written for *Good Housekeeping* Agnes offers advice to girls planning a career in ballet. Since a ballet dancer may not earn a living for three years and may only break even for another six years, Agnes believes a girl should not try to make the grade unless she has some financial backing. As for the requisites—she stresses a strong body because the dancing and travel involved are strenuous. Being reasonably tall and well-proportioned are valuable assets, but poise, grace, dignity, rhythm, a flair for acting and ability to express emotion are more important than body build. Facial expression counts more than beauty. Many a girl has been turned down because of sulkiness.

Alertness, a retentive memory, fast thinking and imagination are important. Because toughness has gone out of fashion in the theater, Agnes thinks directors are looking for wholesome girls. Anyone who plans to be a ballet dancer should cultivate habits of neatness and punctuality.

Music lessons sharpen sensitivity to rhythm, and a broad cultural background is an asset. Concerning college, Agnes says, "I have an enormous regard for the humanities and for university education, but believe that for purely practical reasons it is impossible for performers in any technical medium to avail themselves of four years of college. This is unfortunate but I think the attention of the authorities is being directed toward this predicament."

Because creativeness is slow of growth and recognition, the artist must have faith in and enormous feeling for dancing, not just hazy sentiment. Many dancers are afraid to take risks for what they believe in and end up doing the slick, routine thing for recompense. This attitude, Agnes believes, hurts the whole field of ballet. It also destroys the individual, because no first-class job, whether in dancing or anything else, is ever achieved without a good deal in view besides the check.

A major cause of failure among would-be ballerinas is lack of discipline in scheduling time and handling emotions. Constant daily practice is a necessity, even in the face of frustration or seeming exhaustion.

Agnes' devotion to ballet persisted, and in 1953 The Agnes de Mille Dance Theater toured the United States under the management of Sol Hurok. In the summer of 1956 she was invited to Covent Garden to dance in two of her own works—*Rodeo* and *Three Virgins and a Devil*. That same year Agnes successfuly invaded television, appearing as narrator, dancer, choreographer on *Omnibus,* with a program which portrayed the evolution of ballet style from the seventeenth century to the present, and another on choreography.

Although dancing is her first love, Agnes has other interests. Her articles appear frequently in leading periodicals. She is a trustee of Sarah Lawrence College and of the Henry George School of Social Science. A college, Agnes asserts, should not be considered as a marriage bureau, employment agency, social club or arena. It is a place where standards are maintained and questions asked. "The questions are fundamental—the answers clear, enduring, passionate."

One of Agnes' hobbies is collecting fine china. She has a wonderful theater collection of books, prints and programs. Occasionally she plays tennis with her husband, who is Sol Hurok's assistant. As a family the Prudes enjoy walking and do a great deal of reading aloud together.

In the summer they often go to a home in Sullivan County, New York. There Agnes, who deeply appreciates beauty in nature, spends many hours gardening, although she describes herself as "a wretchedly poor gardener."

Agnes de Mille has had a tremendous influence on American ballet. When she was a student there were no native ballet companies, and Americans in general were indifferent to the art. Only four cities boasted good ballet schools. Pioneering with *Rodeo*, Agnes gave impetus to the Americanization of the Ballet Russe. But she also made old dance techniques say new things. By making ballet understandable to ordinary people, she captured their interest and at the same time raised the level of appreciation. By expanding the range of creative ballet, she helped make more openings for dancers and choreographers.

Agnes says of her success, "This career was not made

without generous and magnificent help." But Agnes did a great deal to help herself. Through fourteen years of reverses, frustration and failure she kept on working without losing her sense of humor or her deep-seated love of dancing. With intense determination, dedication and courage she persisted in setting new standards of perfection—not because she wanted the indirect rewards of fame and fortune, but because she had to express the beauty she knew. Always she found joy in work for its own sake.

Throughout it all Agnes, who sees sheer conformity in the creative arts as the breaking down of the will, in fact death, maintained her integrity and the valor of her own thoughts. In an article titled "Rhythm In My Blood" in *The Atlantic Monthly* she wrote, "One can't go through life on hands and knees. One leaps in the dark." Agnes has done just that. Unwilling to settle for the mediocre, hackneyed or unlovely, she has lived according to standards set by saints and philosophers more than by those set by quick-profit theatrical agents. It is for such standards even more than for her achievements in ballet that the bravos go up for Agnes de Mille.

## 4: FLORENCE ELLINWOOD ALLEN

### A Modern Portia

Several years after Florence Ellinwood Allen had been elected to the Supreme Court of Ohio, the London *Times* carried a story about her. An American tourist saw the picture that had accompanied the article tacked up on the wall of an office in a hotel in the southern part of England. "Why did you save it?" the tourist asked the innkeeper's wife.

"I read the speeches she made up in London, and I like to look at her," the woman told him. "Such folks make life better for all of us."

Judge Florence Allen's ideal has been to make life better through law. First woman to be appointed a county prosecuting attorney in Ohio, first woman ever to sit in a state supreme court, only woman ever to sit in the United States Court of Appeals, she is today the world's most famous woman jurist.

Much that happened in Florence Allen's childhood helped make these firsts possible. She came from a family in love with crossing frontiers. Her father's people, descendants of the renowned Ethan Allen, were among the first thousand settlers in the Territory of Ohio. On her mother's side of the family, the Fullers, directly descended from Dr. Samuel Fuller of *Mayflower* fame, migrated to Ohio in ox-drawn covered wagons.

When her father was ordered to make a change of climate because he had contracted tuberculosis, Mr. Allen left his position as Professor of Greek and Latin at Western Reserve University and moved the family to Salt Lake City. There he became a mining engineer, helped establish public schools and served as Utah's first congressman. Florence was born in Salt Lake City on March 23, 1884.

For a time the Allens lived in an adobe house that served as a homestead, but later they moved into a big, rambling, frame house. Florence, along with two brothers and three sisters, grew up in a healthy, happy home atmosphere. Salt Lake City in the 1880's was somewhat primitive—there was no city water system, no public school. But with the kind of parents they had, the Allen children never suffered any educational lacks. Mr. Allen tutored them in Latin and Greek, which Florence could read when she was four, having learned the Greek alphabet for her father's birthday present.

At Salt Lake College, a private Congregational school, Florence was an outstanding student. Because of a childhood ambition to be an architect, she studied mechanical drawing on the side.

Mrs. Allen, who had been a student at Smith College the first year the school opened, supervised the musical activities of the girls. Florence played piano. Her sister Elizabeth played cello, and Esther not only mastered the violin, but worked out elaborate trio arrangements. The three girls provided a lot of entertainment for themselves as well as for others. On summer evenings friends and neighbors would come and sit on the large Allen veranda to listen while the sisters performed.

The Allens also enjoyed song fests together. They compiled their own collection of ditties written by various members of the family for birthdays and special holidays. One of their favorites was about their father, who had grown up on a farm. This began with, "Father rose at 2 A.M., stars he really was a gem." The song went on to describe the deeds and experiences of the farm boy who became a congressman.

All of the Allen children delighted in hiking and climbing the mountains around Salt Lake City. Once when Florence was about twelve the youngsters with some older friends had set out to climb North Black Mountain, a high ridge behind the city. Undeterred when they lost the trail, they persisted in climbing upward through almost impenetrable brush. It was six o'clock before they finally reached the top. They came over the ridge into a canyon, which had a rough road running through it. Florence was so tired from all the walking and pushing through brush that she lay down in the road, saying any wagon that came along could run over her.

Luckily the moon came out and the children made their way down on the side hill to town and caught the last streetcar home, but Florence was so tired and lame her mother had to help her undress and bathe.

One of the Allens' family customs was reading aloud together or telling stories. Their favorite was about an Indian raid in the early days in Ohio. A grandparent, a baby at the time, had been spared because his mother had hidden him behind a log when the alarm was given and the Indians didn't find him. The mother, however, was killed.

Among the books the family read together, Florence liked the *Odyssey* best. Her persistent and analytical questions, "Who planned what to do?" or "What about the women and children?" made her father remark to Mrs. Allen, "If she were a boy I'd know she would study law."

Intellectually, Florence was ready for college at fourteen, but her parents wanted her to wait until she was
sixteen. This gave her a chance to practice piano intensively. She then went East to attend New Lyme Institute
in Ohio, then entered Western Reserve University, from
which she was graduated in 1904 with high honors.

During the next two years Florence studied music in
Berlin, Germany. While preparing for a lecture which
she planned to illustrate by playing some very technical
Chopin studies, she suffered a severe nerve injury to her
arm. She could still play, but it became apparent that the
constant practicing necessary for a professional musician
would overtax her arm.

Florence met the experience as a challenge. "I can't
remember being too upset," she comments. "There were
so many other things I was interested in."

The time had not been wasted—the habit of self-discipline imposed by serious music study, along with the appreciation and inspiration she had gained, carried over
into later life.

Upon her return to the United States, Florence served
on the staff of the Cleveland *Plain Dealer* as music critic.
She also taught music at the Laurel School, and lectured.
Her remarkable linguistic abilities were put to use
through translations. Under the title of *Patris*, a Greek
word meaning fatherland, she published a book of poetry.

Florence could have had a career in journalism, music
or education, but an interest which had always run deep
in the Allen family was stirring within her—concern for
public welfare. She decided she wanted to be a lawyer. In
the early 1900's such a decision meant clearing many
hurdles, not least of which would be finding a law school
that would accept a woman.

To get a sampling of some of the subjects she would

need as a lawyer, Florence re-entered Western Reserve University, where she earned an M.A. in political science and constitutional law. The subject matter had fascinated her, but despite her brilliant scholastic record the university refused to enroll her in its law school.

But once Florence had made up her mind, she was not a person to give up easily or to scatter her objectives. Since she wanted to be a lawyer, she took definite, logical steps toward that goal and finally succeeded in wedging her way into the University of Chicago Law School. From Chicago she went on to New York University, where she was the first woman to receive an LL.D. degree. To earn her way through law school she lectured on current topics.

In 1914 Florence was admitted to the Ohio Bar and opened an office in Cleveland. Her preparation for her career had been unusually thorough and she had an all out dedication to law, but because she was a woman all the usual difficulties of getting established were doubled. Finding she had spare time on her hands, Florence volunteered as counselor for the Legal Aid Society. She also was asked to handle the legal work for the Women's Suffrage Party. Florence had for some time been an ardent champion of equal rights for women. In addition to the legal help she gave, she did a lot of public speaking in behalf of suffrage for women.

Once she was to make a very important speech at a theater in Toledo, Ohio. A wealthy and prominent suffragette sent her a very elegant light-blue dress for the occasion. At the hotel where she was staying, Florence was baffled as to how to put the gown on and hired a maid to help her. Then she went on to make a successful appearance at the theater.

Later, when thanking her friend for the beautiful gown,

which Florence felt had contributed to audience respon-
siveness, she learned to her horror that she had worn the
dress backside front. The incident may have made her a
little more clothes-conscious. Today Judge Allen dresses
with excellent taste, although milliners sometimes sigh
over the way she treats a hat.

As a young lawyer Florence represented the women of
East Cleveland, who had induced the men responsible for
framing a new city charter for that municipality to include
a provision giving women the right to vote in city elections. The charter containing this provision was adopted
but the Board of Elections of Cuyahoga County refused
to permit women to vote in the next municipal election.
In consequence the Woman Suffrage Party of Cuyahoga
County instituted a mandamus case in the Supreme Court
of Ohio, praying for an order which would compel the
Board of Elections to permit women to vote in East Cleveland.

It was the first time a woman had argued before this
court and there was considerable skepticism in legal circles. Those who were in the courtroom saw a quiet, competent woman with naturally wavy hair and keen blue
eyes, who spoke directly and forcefully in a clear, beautifully modulated voice. Because she knew judges were strict
about lawyers' keeping to the time allotted, Florence com-
plied. But when she finished she said, "I wish I had more
time to explain this to you."

Leaning over the bench Judge Donahue said in a kindly
tone, "Take five more minutes." Not until later did Florence realize how remarkable it was that he permitted her
overtime.

Supplementing her activities both in and out of the
court in behalf of women's suffrage, Florence crusaded for

peace. Her anti-war sentiments were intensified when her oldest brother, who had taken every conceivable honor at Yale University, both scholastic and athletic, was killed in action. A second brother, also extremely gifted, died as a result of injuries received during combat.

In 1918 Florence became Assistant Prosecutor for Cuyahoga County—the first woman to hold such a position in Ohio. When presenting a case she was poised and natural, exhibiting no fidgety motions or nervous gestures. And her cool-headed address to a jury was straight and simple. But it was also apparent that underneath her judicial competence lay warmth and sensitivity to a client's need. Florence saw the court not just as a place for interpreting statutes, meting out punishments or settling controversies, but as a place for administering the people's will. It was her belief that laws and courts should not only protect society, but contribute to every person's safety, peace and happiness.

After ratification of the Nineteenth Amendment, which gave women the right to vote, women of Cleveland urged Florence to run for judge. A year after her appointment as Assistant Prosecutor, she was elected Judge of the Court of Common Pleas by the largest majority vote ever given a judicial candidate for that court.

Soon after this, a case involving theft came to the court. When Judge Allen found that the thief was out on bail while a prosecuting witness had lain in jail for weeks through the heat of the summer, she was very indignant. According to Ohio law nothing could prevent such hardships from being inflicted on other innocent victims. Judge Allen could have said, "I'm a woman and just getting started in law; I'd better let this alone." Instead, she made up her mind to change the unjust law by which witnesses could be detained. Her creative imagination conjured up ways and means of accomplishing this. Spurred by the belief that when people know the facts about injustice they care, and when they care they act, Judge Allen spoke at various meetings, setting off a chain reaction. Clubs and newspapers took up the crusade and the Cleveland Foundation launched a survey of courts and procedures. In the end an aroused public put through the desired legislation.

Judge Allen saw no reason why the Ten Commandments should not be applied to public as well as to personal life. Although she knew it might cost her something in personal popularity, she sent a judge to prison for perjury. Lawyers and judges, she argued, were civil servants. If they were inefficient, incompetent or immoral, they should be removed from office.

When Judge Allen was elected to the State Supreme Court in 1922, she became the first woman in the world to sit in a court of last resort. To the post she brought a fine sense of justice and impartiality. By word and deed she proved to those who had objections to woman judges that she could uphold the honor and dignity of the court. There might be a gay print dress with feminine frills under her somber black robe, but while sitting in the courtroom she was all judge and her customarily genial face remained sober. However, it soon became clear that Judge Allen cared more that the court be just and honest than that it be sacred. Eager to keep people from thinking of justice as a legal chess game she encouraged people to visit the courts and offer constructive criticism.

Although neither sentimental nor indulgent, Judge Allen disliked sending a criminal to prison. She would have favored diagnosing a case, finding out what was wrong, and then sentencing the defendant in such a way that he would be able to earn his livelihood and develop his best traits and talents. Despite her belief that punishment did not make people better, she never shrank from doing her duty. But her love of social justice showed through in her careful, honest decisions. "Law is one of man's important tools to promote better living together," she often said.

Judge Allen's lack of bias and prejudice in her decisions, her court reforms, her philosophy that courts existed for protection rather than for vengeance attracted attention nationally and internationally. In 1926 Smith College, where Florence's mother had graduated, conferred an honorary LL.D. degree upon her. Two years later she ran for reelection to the Supreme Court of Ohio on an independent ticket. She won by a majority of about 350,000 votes.

In 1934 President Franklin D. Roosevelt appointed Florence Allen as Judge, United States Court of Appeals for the Sixth Circuit, which includes Ohio, Michigan, Kentucky, Tennessee. Thus she became the first and only woman in the world ever to serve in such a capacity. This court, second in importance only to the United States Supreme Court, deals with such matters as patents, taxes, labor controversies, personal injuries, stolen cars, contracts, bankruptcy and narcotics. The appointment meant hard work. The United States Sixth Circuit ranked fourth in the nation in volume of work handled. One day Judge Allen's desk might be piled high with data and rulings on power plants, the next with facts on a drug case or the parts of some mechanical device involved in a patent dispute.

Much of the technical subject matter would have baffled

most women, but Judge Allen amazed her colleagues by her grasp of cases. Always she read in advance the case briefs, which despite their name are anything but brief, and appeared in the courtroom well informed. Two techniques helped her to get through a phenomenal amount of material in a relatively short time. The first was her remarkable capacity to read a page practically at a glance and to extract the most salient points. The second was her unusual ability to concentrate. Even so, she very much dislikes being interrupted while working.

For Judge Allen appointment to the federal bench meant giving up personal crusades—even the championship of peace. Because judges must not appear to be prejudiced they are forbidden to express opinions on important or controversial issues. Other sacrifices were involved, such as periodically leaving her pleasant home in Cleveland and living in a hotel room during sessions of the circuit court, which met in Cincinnati. But law is her love and she has never complained over the inconveniences involved.

As a Circuit Court Judge, Florence Allen has made a distinguished record. She has exhibited strength not only of body, but of mind and character, crossing legal frontiers. In 1936 a new woman's party invited her to become a candidate for the presidency of the United States. Her refusal was emphatic. Chi Omega sorority chose her in 1938 to be recipient of their national award given annually to women whose achievements are considered worthy of honor.

Outside the courtroom Judge Allen has many activities and varied contacts, but they have been subordinated to the big interest in her life—law. With a dog, or sometimes several of them for companions, she has a comfortable, attractive home filled with books, but she doesn't go in for domesticity. The inroads made on her at-home time by work on legal documents and the mountains of mail coming her way leave little energy for cooking, sewing or shopping, in which she has less than average interest anyway.

Occasionally Judge Allen entertains, but usually informally—often with steaks broiled in the fireplace. Because she plays as wholeheartedly as she works, she is a comfortable person to be with and a gentle mannered, congenial hostess. Her deep infectious laugh is proof of her enjoyment of the lighter side of life.

Although her intense concentration on law leaves Judge Allen little time for serious piano practice, she does play enough to keep on giving creditable performances of her favorite composers—Beethoven and Schumann. Her prodigious memory carries over into poetry. All her life Judge Allen has at odd intervals memorized poems, and what she has learned never seems to be forgotten.

Judge Allen enjoys gardening and walking in woods, mountains or meadows. For years a brisk walk at daybreak has been part of her daily routine. Even when staying at the hotel in Cincinnati she strides off down the city streets as dawn breaks between the tall buildings.

Judge Allen is active in community affairs, but never permits them to detract from her dedication to law. For many years she has been a member of the Euclid Avenue Congregational Church of Cleveland. Her deep faith in the American home has caused her to support legal measures benefitting mothers and children. She has frequently quoted her mother as saying: "The roots of all good things are in the home." Her own family ties have always meant much to Judge Allen. While she was judge of the Ohio Supreme Court she lived with her parents, who came to make a home for her in Columbus. After their death, Judge Allen often spent week-ends in the old home with her sister, Esther Allen Gaw, who was for many years Dean of Women at Ohio State University.

After the death of a soldier brother, Judge Allen became guardian of his thirteen-year-old daughter. For this youngster she would push aside technical briefs and thoughts of judgeship to become simply Aunt Florence.

A student of constitutional history, Judge Allen in 1938 published a book titled *This Constitution of Ours*. The theme is that all of us should be familiar with the Constitution and its guarantees. Although scholarly, the book is written in a clear, crisp style. "Each generation must create liberty for its own times," writes Judge Allen. "We must practice the principle that all men are in essential nature alike."

About the book Dr. Harlan Hatcher, then Professor of English at Ohio State University, said, "It will make every man and woman, every boy and girl more erect in spirit for the reading."

Judge Allen's able work on the Circuit Court and her brave book have brought distinction and numerous awards. Twenty-two colleges and universities have given her an LL.D. degree, among them Washington University at St. Louis, New York University, Western Reserve University, Mount Holyoke College, Ohio Wesleyan University and Rutgers University. At George Washington University in Washington, D. C., she was made honorary member of the Order of The Coif. The National Federation of Business and Professional Women selected her as the leading professional woman in America. In May 1952 she was chosen to deliver the Susan B. Anthony address at the Hall of Fame in Washington, D. C.

Acclaim has not made Judge Allen pompous. Modesty

seems to be a family trait. At a reception in Florence's honor, her mother listened to the gushing superlatives of a guest, then said quietly, "Yes, Florence is a nice girl."

Judge Allen has concerned herself with every struggle for liberty and justice, whether at home or elsewhere in the world. She has addressed many national conventions such as the Conference on the Causes and Cures of War, established by Carrie Chapman Catt, and national programs of the League of Women Voters.

In 1950 Judge Allen presided at the Section on Human Rights at the International Bar Association Convention in London. Two years later she presided at an International Bar Association in Madrid, and at the Section on International Law at the International Federation of Women Lawyers at Istanbul, Turkey. While she was abroad her command of Latin, Greek, French and Spanish stood her in good stead.

At Washington, D. C., in 1957, Judge Allen represented the United States Court of Appeals for the Sixth Circuit at the conference of the National Judicial Council of the Federal Courts—another first for a woman.

Today more than four thousand women are in active law practice. Asked for advice to girls interested in entering the profession, Judge Allen pointed out the necessity of realizing that the preparation is long. Beyond college with its general background of philosophy, Latin, history, science, and the humanities, several more years will be required for specialization in government, economics, constitutional law. And then there is the likelihood of several years in which income will not match necessary expenditures. "No girl," Judge Allen cautions, "should enter the profession of law who is not prepared to go through with this long period of waiting and also to work very hard, for the law is an arduous mistress." As a recipe for success in law she suggests, "Take one generous dose of persistency. Add one large measure of industry—the kind that takes no thought of dances, evening parties or prolonged vacations. Mix thoroughly and season with a good portion of humor and several ounces of tact—and don't be emotional."

Judge Allen has followed her own recipe. With tireless industry she has directed her ambition and energy to a single goal. In love with law, she has whole-heartedly given her life to it. Although a most compassionate person, she does not yield to run-away emotions. In and out of court her tact and sense of humor have often extricated her from tense situations.

A sample of her humor is the title of a speech given in 1956 before the Cincinnati Business and Professional Women's Club, which Judge Allen helped to organize in 1919: "Our Get Up and Go and Where It's Been."

Another factor in Judge Allen's success has been her intellectual curiosity. It began with her keen, analytical questions about the *Odyssey*. It has never diminished. Judge Allen is not content until she has plumbed the depths of a subject. Because she is always probing for reasons why, her intellectual horizons are constantly expanding.

Orderly, purposeful, methodical, Judge Allen plans what she wants to do and then does it. She has a definite schedule for work, exercise, sleep. If bedtime is nine o'clock, she holds to it. No exceptions clutter her program. Even when busiest she is never late for appointments, yet she never seems to be rushed.

Her outstanding integrity has been maintained even when it required a lonely kind of courage. This is more than a strict code of ethics. Any dishonesty of thought is completely alien to her. Integrity has been buttressed by the mental and moral courage to take a stand she feels is right no matter how unpopular it may be. Adding warmth to Judge Allen's courage and integrity has been her genuine and abiding interest in people and their problems. To humanize law and make it serve society by promoting justice and better, happier living for everyone has been her ideal. Because of her common-sense approach and her ability to inspire, she has sparked others to go and do likewise.

No wonder First to do this-or-that has so often been written after Judge Florence Allen's name. Upright and able, she has opened doors heretofore closed to women and has become the greatest Portia of our day. But in addition to being a fearless fighter for social justice, she is a poised and serene woman who shows a marked sensitivity to the true and the beautiful whether in music, poetry or people. Of Judge Florence Allen a friend has said, "All about her is a little pool of peace."

# 5: KATHARINE CORNELL

## A *Migrant Juliet*

At the age of ten Katharine Cornell saw Maude Adams in *Peter Pan* and was greatly impressed. Some days later she calmly told her mother, "I'm going to be an actress."

Mrs. Cornell looked down at the leggy, awkward child with a long braid tied in a crisp taffeta ribbon and said gently, "Perhaps you will change your mind."

Katharine was sure she wouldn't. A dream had claimed her, a dream which, coupled with faith and intense application, would one day establish her as a first lady of the theater. She also became the first actress to succeed in taking serious drama on the road.

Much in Katharine's childhood influenced her toward a career on the stage. At the time of her birth in Berlin, Germany, on February 16, 1898, her father was a doctor taking a post-graduate course in surgery. But drama was his great love and he was an excellent amateur actor. Talented Grandfather Cornell spent most of his time directing plays in a small theater in his home that was completely equipped with stage, lights, screen curtains. Almost the first words in Katharine's vocabulary were show, cue, stage.

Although Mrs. Cornell, a strikingly attractive woman with lovely hazel eyes, had no dramatic inclinations, she graciously lent support to her gifted, energetic family. Kit, as she was usually called, was deeply loyal to her warm-hearted, vital mother.

The Cornell home was an interesting place in which to grow up, never lacking in a generous supply of clothes, toys and gymnastic equipment. Tempted by the many books surrounding her, Kit learned to appreciate the best in literature. But she also looked forward to expeditions with her jolly, vigorous father.

Once, when she was about five, Dr. Cornell, as a special reward, took her to a vaudeville theater where elephants were being featured. Kit, who had anticipated the event for days, took a bag of buns to feed the animals. But for some reason she had pictured elephants as being dog-sized, and when she saw the huge, lumbering animals, she was terrified and begged her father to take her home. Dr. Cornell, a believer in finishing anything that was undertaken, insisted that she place one of her buns in a gray, writhing trunk. Discipline from a parent in this and similar instances instilled in Kit such qualities as perseverance, reliability and courage.

A restless, active child, Kit enjoyed the Cornells' summer home in Cobourg, Ontario, where she picked flowers, swam, rode horseback and played tennis proficiently. She also wrote plays about queens and princesses which she staged in the long gallery at the back of the house. It was not at all unusual for Kit to insist on playing several parts —including the villian.

When Dr. Cornell decided to quit medicine and buy the Majestic Theater in Buffalo, Kit's major interest was roller skating in the big foyer that had a smooth, sloped floor. Fearless and agile, she spent many hours climbing trees, playing basketball, riding a bike, exercising on gym equipment in the back yard until she became so adept on the trapeze that at the age of ten she was invited to perform at a charity circus.

There Kit saw a tightrope walker. Touched by her admiration of his act, the performer gave her a slack wire that was strung in the back yard. Driven by the ambition to join a circus, Kit conscientiously practiced walking the tightrope and became the envy of her playmates.

But moody, oversensitive, high-tempered Kit sometimes found it difficult to adjust to schoolmates. Older looking, and in some ways older acting than other children of her own age, she was extremely shy and tended to avoid rather than seek companionship.

At school everything interested her except mathematics. Receptive and quick to learn, she was forever asking questions. She had a remarkably retentive memory and loved learning parts for school plays or pageants.

Then came the day Kit was to see Maude Adams in *Peter Pan*. Sitting beside Mrs. Cornell in the theater, she fussed and fidgeted in anticipation.

"Sh-h-h," whispered her mother. "The curtain is going up."

There was nothing more exciting, thought Kit, than that marvelous hush just before a play began.

*Peter Pan* left Kit living in a world of enchantment. The time had come, she told herself, for putting aside roller skates, baseballs and jacks. She was going to become an actress. Kit wasn't exactly sure about how people got to be actresses, but she intended to find out.

Part of her program of finding out was attendance at rehearsals in her father's theater. Kit quickly learned theatrical jargon—foots, flies, props. And when the manager would say—"This plank is a piano," she had no trouble picturing it as such.

What fascinated her the most was the way an actress could be just an ordinary person one minute, and the next minute be a queen, a Juliet or a Joan of Arc. She would look at the exotic people and wonder if they had ever been afraid of elephants or climbed trees or fallen off tightropes. Kit decided she loved everything about the theater, the confusion and clatter—even the smell.

Actress and producer Jessie Bonstelle, who regularly brought her stock shows to Buffalo, took a friendly interest in the pale-faced child with the dark, intelligent eyes often seen at rehearsal time. "Hurry and grow up and play Jo for me," she said one day.

Kit knew that before she could play Jo she'd have to get over her shyness. There were other handicaps, too. You're too homely and awkward, she would tell herself as she peered in her mirror comparing her wide cheek bones and straight hair with the profiles of the beautiful, confident-looking women on the posters in the Majestic Theater. Avidly she read every book she could find on plays and actresses, probing for secrets of their success. One of her most prized possessions was a biography of the great Sarah Bernhardt. However, she didn't completely abandon athletics as she had once planned. Runner-up for the Buffalo championship in tennis, she was also the city's amateur swimming champion.

When Kit was sixteen she went to Oaksmere, a preparatory school in Mamaroneck, Long Island. She enjoyed her courses, especially psychology, which helped her learn how to deal with people and situations. But clinging tenaciously to her dream of becoming an actress, she concentrated on drama, taking very little time out for social life. Her muscles, well-developed through athletics, served her well, as did her full, beautiful, well-modulated voice. Kit's imagination and facile memorization were assets, but it was difficult for her to project her emotions into an audience.

Because she thought actresses should be interested in people and be graciously at ease, she tried to force herself to talk to strangers.

Two years after she enrolled at Oaksmere her mother died suddenly. At first Kit, who loved her mother devotedly, had difficulty making an adjustment. Without Mrs. Cornell's encouragement, love and understanding, she felt restless. For comfort she turned again to drama. Kit not only acted in plays but wrote and directed them—mostly pantomimes or allegorical plays about vestal virgins with holy fire or Alexander the Great and the captive maiden. To coach one of her dramatic works titled simply *Play,* the school called in Edward Goodman of the Washington Square Players. The girls, including Kit, stood in awe of the short, dark man with a mustache, who was making a name as a director.

As Goodman was leaving Oaksmere he said casually, "If you're thinking of going into the theater, let me know when you come to New York." To Kit, who was thinking of little else, the brief, hurried words were a golden promise.

When her days at Oaksmere were over she announced her intention of going to New York to become an actress. Although interested, Dr. Cornell refused to take her intentions seriously. "Jobs are irregular," he told Kit," and the work is hard."

Aunt Lucy Plimpton, who regarded the theater as immoral and unladylike, was openly worried and resisted the idea of eighteen-year-old Kit's going to the big city on her own. Actress acquaintances dwelt on the uncertainties and sacrifices—giving up dates, a home, a private life.

But Kit's dream persisted. What did she care about hardships? Acting was something high and fine—it would be worth the sacrifices. Overcoming objections, she took the small allowance coming to her from her mother's estate and with high hopes set off for New York. As soon as she was settled in a boarding house, Aunt Lucy came to keep a watchful eye on her.

Kit expected to serve a period of apprenticeship before she broke into the world of footlights and applause, but she also expected a helping hand from Edward Goodman, although it had been a year and a half since their meeting at Oaksmere. She hurried eagerly to Goodman's office in the Comedy Theater. There she sat for three hours in the crowded waiting room. Finally Goodman, looking very preoccupied, came out of his office, but he brushed by her without any sign of recognition. For a person with Kit's sensitivity it took courage to come back to Goodman's office, but she kept reappearing. As the weeks passed with no summons and it dawned on her that Goodman hadn't meant what he said, Kit became more hurt and disappointed.

But one day Goodman stopped beside her and said, "Some people are going to read. If you'd like to try, come along."

Kit's heart beat like a tom-tom. Her knees were shaky, her body taut. When her time came to go on stage she took the script and read in a stifled voice.

"Louder," boomed Mr. Goodman.

Kit tried, but by now she was so nervous that her voice wouldn't function at all.

"Sorry," Mr. Goodman told her. "You won't do."

Crushed and disheartened, Kit stumbled out into the street. Here's the chance you've been waiting for, she told herself as she walked along in a fury of self-condemnation, and you let fear defeat you. Finding herself in front of a church she went in and sat crying away her depression. Something inside her suggested that she give up and go home. But the dream wouldn't die. In desperation Kit sent for Dr. Cornell.

"Couldn't you get someone to coach you?" he asked.

Thinking over the possibilities, Kit decided to approach Florence Enright who had coached a play at Oaksmere and who had also spoken to Kit kindly on the day of the try-outs at the Comedy Theater.

Touched by Kit's courage and her humble willingness to learn, Miss Enright agreed to coach her, but warned, "It's going to take a lot of self-discipline. You'll have to get over your shyness and self-consciousness."

Kit didn't care how much discipline she would have to undergo if it would make her an actress. Working with painstaking thoroughness and deep receptivity, she learned to think less about Kit Cornell and more about the character she was portraying. There were times when the gnawing fear that she wasn't good enough writhed inside her, but she didn't surrender to it. At Miss Enright's suggestion she attended rehearsals of the Washington Square Players being directed by Goodman. Day after day she arrived punctually and took a back seat in the Comedy Theater. She watched intently and learned all she could.

One morning at rehearsals of a play with a Japanese setting called *Bushido,* the girl assigned to the part of the mother failed to appear. Goodman turned and saw the forever-expectant Kit. "Here," he barked. "Read this for me."

Eagerly Kit reached for the script. After she had read Goodman said, "You'll do."

The part consisted of only four words, "My son! My son!" The actress who had skipped rehearsal considered it too trivial to work on. But Kit, who was never half-hearted about any role, seized the opportunity gratefully. She repeated the words as she walked along the street. At home she practiced them over and over to get the right inflection, the right body attitude. At the next rehearsal she did so well that Goodman gave her the part for keeps.

Kit didn't care that the part was so minor or that there was no pay for playing it. She was in. She would now be considered one of the Washington Square Players, a group of ambitious, semi-professional young people whose originality had impressed even hard-boiled critics.

Unusually responsive to direction, exact, painstaking Kit got her first real part in *Plots and Playwrights*. Although Kit had not yet conquered stage fright, she lost her nervousness when the footlights went on and played her role very creditably. However, Broadway producers paid no attention.

Mrs. Frances M. Wolcott, long a friend of the Cornell family, tried to give Kit a boost by seeing that she met influential people. At a dinner party staged for this purpose, Kit was miserably self-conscious and afterwards felt that her blunders must surely have made an unfavorable impression—especially on the Favershams who were people with prestige in the world of the theater.

When the Comedy Theater closed for the summer, Kit went to Buffalo to be with her father. Quite unexpectedly,

William Faversham telegraphed and suggested that she try out for the lead in his new play. Kit wanted that part, but she knew she was too young and inexperienced. Reluctantly, she wired a refusal.

During her second season with the Washington Square Players, Kit earned forty dollars, won her first special mention from *The New York Times* in the play *Blind Alleys,* and got a role in Zona Gale's *Neighbors.*

Hours of rehearsal were long and often trying, and Kit's growth was slow, but although she had daydreamed about acting she had never entertained the fatuous idea that stardom could come without preparation and training. In fact, she wasn't much interested in becoming a star —being a good enough actress to make the audience feel what you felt was what counted.

Whole-heartedly interested in others, devoid of professional jealousy, Kit found the Washington Square Players almost as stimulating off-stage as on-stage. For hours on end they talked about everything from their personal plans to World War I and its effect on drama.

One night when Kit was playing in *Neighbors* there was a knock at her dressing room door. "Miss Bonstelle!" cried Kit when she saw the smartly dressed, dynamic woman who had been her stock show friend in her father's theater.

"Want to join my show in Buffalo this summer?" Miss Bonstelle asked. "Fifth business."

Fifth business meant that Kit would be expected to play small parts—anything from a maid to a witch. But she knew that most of the world's greatest actresses had gotten a start that way and that the experience would be invaluable. "I'd love to," she said.

Kit worked harder than she had ever worked in her

life. Ten performances a week and a new play every Monday night meant a lot of memorization of roles. And no one handed Kit her costumes. She had to find them for herself. Since she couldn't sew she borrowed or bought most of them, the result being that she spent more than she earned.

Dr. Cornell expected that Kit would soon tire of the grind, but after fourteen plays in Buffalo she went on with the show to Detroit.

Jessie Bonstelle was a strict disciplinarian. Everyone had to study, work hard and be on time, but most of the cast cooperated willingly. Kit's worst trouble was that her roles, though minor, demanded versatility and adaptability, and her first reading was almost always bad. But because she listened intelligently and was both pliable and patient, she ended up with good public appearances. Wilted by heat, she shuttled back and forth between the hot, stuffy, dusty theater and a small, dingy hotel room, with almost no time out for diversion. The summer's experiences taught Kit a great deal about the techniques of acting, and she gained in poise, self-confidence and a slow, easy grace. Her arresting individuality, her ability to project her voice and emotions convinced Miss Bonstelle that Kit had a brilliant future. An important by-product for Kit was learning that one has to work harmoniously with people and help them develop if one is to grow as an actress and as a person. Moreover, Kit, who had a tendency to procrastinate, learned to do what was important right on schedule.

When the stock show closed, Kit went back to New York. There she found that World War I had folded the Washington Square Players. In one crowded casting office after another, footsore and weary, she sat or stood for

hours only to get answers like, "Too tall . . . Too young
. . . Sorry, we want a blonde." But even when all doors
seemed closed to her, Kit loved the stage more than anything else.

Then out of the blue, Jessie Bonstelle called, "Can you
be at the Playhouse tomorrow?"

Could she!

But next morning when Kit saw the part was a swiftly-
paced comedy, her excitement oozed away.

Miss George, for whom she read, said, "You don't think
you can play the part, do you, Miss Cornell? You're not
the type."

Kit thought Miss George was dismissing her. She left
by the stage entrance. Lonely and wretched, she walked
dejectedly down the alley. Wanting to get as far as possible
from the scene of her failure, she decided to go to Washington to get a car a friend had been wanting driven to
New York. She told no one of her plans.

When she returned to her New York apartment she
found that Miss Bonstelle had been frantic with worry
over her whereabouts.

Miss Bonstelle also scolded Kit for walking out of a rehearsal without being properly dismissed. "Miss George
wanted you back for a second reading," she told her. "But
the way you handled it made her think you don't have
the right stuff."

The incident made Kit face herself honestly. Instead of
wasting her time on self-justification, she acknowledged
that she was too sensitive, too quick to jump to conclu-
sions. After this she'd have the courage to stick it out as
long as there was any chance at all.

Once more she doggedly made the rounds of the casting offices. Convinced that Kit had learned a valuable

lesson, the generous Miss Bonstelle got her a chance in the road show, *The Man Who Came Back*. It meant catching trains at 4 A.M. often in zero weather, second-rate hotels, poor food, drafty dressing rooms. But Kit loved getting to be in the play.

That summer Kit went to Buffalo and Detroit again with Jessie Bonstelle. By the end of the summer she was so bone-tired and weary that she became obsessed with the idea of simply stretching out and doing nothing for days and days.

When Miss Bonstelle offered her the part of Jo in London performances, Kit replied, "I need a vacation."

"Not at all," Miss Bonstelle told her, and hustled her off to England. Rehearsals went badly. Miss Bonstelle was harsh and critical. Smarting under the rebuke and ridicule, Kit was in turn sulky and rebellious. But her inner hurt was released after Miss Bonstelle confessed that she had a deep affection for Kit and was rigid and exacting only because she wanted her to become a truly great actress.

Critics acclaimed Kit's portrayal of Jo, the awkward but honest and sensitive tomboy. But the conditions under which Kit was living detracted somewhat from the elation of her success. The only American in the cast, she was often lonely. Her intensive dramatic work left little time or energy for cultivating a social life or for recreation, although she did some golfing. Spending Christmas in a cold room away from home and friends intensified her loneliness, and she was glad to sail for America in February.

The following summer Kit again went to Detroit with the Bonstelle show. In charge of rehearsals at the old Gar-

rick Theater was youthful Guthrie McClintic. Kit admired
his enthusiasm, energy and idealism—obviously he was
going places as a director. It soon became apparent that
the frank, friendly Guthrie believed in Kit's future, but
he was sometimes as hard to please as Miss Bonstelle. Because Kit saw that his criticisms were logical and intelligent, she worked to overcome her diffidence.

Seeking relief from a heat wave which daily made ther-
mometers register between ninety-two and a hundred and
four degrees, Kit and Guthrie went to the park one afternoon. Talking about their strenuous but exciting life, they
found they had similar ideas. Both loved the high and
beautiful things in the theater; both were striving for perfection.

Unending rehearsals left little time for romancing, but
the young lovers snatched brief hours for rides or a walk
in the park. After Guthrie confessed he had been in love
with her ever since he had seen her one day in a casting
office, Kit had trouble keeping her mind on her work.

Jessie Bonstelle, seeing the effect the emotional up-
heaval had on Kit's acting, disapproved of the romance
violently. Marriage, she was convinced, could wreck Kit's
future. Kit, however, felt sure she could make a go of both
marriage and a career.

At the end of the summer she returned to New York
but had no luck in the casting offices. Five years since she
had first come to the city, she thought as she wearily
climbed stairways, and still no real part on Broadway.
Guthrie, to whom she was now engaged, kept telling her
something would turn up, but for seven months she got
tedious rebuffs.

Kit lived for the week-ends when she and Guthrie often

went to the country or seashore for a swim and picnic. Basking in the sun they usually read a script or talked of their plans for marriage.

After a time Kit got the part of a wisecracking, sophisticated girl in *Nice People*. Although the play was a hit, Kit's role was minor and attracted very little attention.

Then very unexpectedly Kit was offered the role of Sydney in *A Bill of Divorcement*. The chance came to her because English actor Allan Pollock, who had bought American rights to the play, had seen Kit in the part of Jo in London and had confidence in her ability.

Not knowing the exact date for the first rehearsal of *A Bill of Divorcement*, Kit and Guthrie decided to go ahead with their plans for their wedding September 8, 1921. On the third, Kit left the cast of *Nice People* and took the train for her Aunt Lydia's home in Cobourg, Ontario. When Guthrie got there the day of the wedding, he told Kit rehearsals for *A Bill of Divorcement* would begin the next day. They had planned on a short honeymoon, but not that short. However, having long since agreed that each would be left free to pursue his career, and that work and rehearsals would come ahead of romancing, the couple accepted the situation philosophically.

Next morning Kit appeared at the rehearsal full of anticipation, but also fearful that she couldn't do justice to the role of the slightly mad Sydney. Rehearsals were exhausting. Basil Dean, although a top-ranking English director, was not very sympathetic toward Kit and seemed to want a carbon copy reproduction of the London performance of the play.

To the terrific strain of rehearsals was added that of househunting. A big old house on Beekman Place appealed to Kit and Guthrie, but it was in what was then practically a slum district. The fact that the property had garden space, was on the East River, and afforded a view of the river and of Queensboro Bridge made them decide to rent it. Since the house was not immediately available, they took rooms at the Hotel Chatham.

On the opening night of *A Bill of Divorcement,* Kit barely touched her dinner. Despite telegrams, flowers and moral support from Guthrie, Kit was jittery. There were to be four other openings that night. But by the time she went on stage, Kit was quiet and self-possessed. Although the crowd was small the applause seemed genuine, and Kit had a curtain call—her first alone.

But next morning, a dark, cloudy one, Kit had to steel herself as Guthrie spread newspapers out on the bed. The reviews by the few critics who had seen the play were lukewarm. "The show is doomed," Kit told Guthrie.

But ardent playgoer Carl Van Vechten liked the play and called Alexander Woollcott, theatrical critic of *The New York Times.* "See *A Bill of Divorcement,*" he urged.

"A must." Woollcott wrote afterwards. Other critics went, saw, and were conquered, writing enthusiastically about Katharine Cornell's "slender, dark beauty," her "poetic and haunting voice." *A Bill of Divorcement* had a long run. Hailed as a star of the future, Kit had emerged from obscurity.

Late in October Kit and Guthrie moved into the house on Beekman Place and settled into domestic routines. Their furnishings were scanty but they had plenty of room.

Kit, who had agonized with Guthrie over the difficulties he had had breaking into production, wept with joy when he was given a chance as director of *The Dover Road,* which drew rave notices.

When *A Bill of Divorcement* closed after a long run, the McClintics traveled to Munich, Venice, Prague and England on money Guthrie had made in producing *The Dover Road*. While abroad they were continually discussing new plays, new techniques, higher achievements. Kit, who always had a great sense of responsibility to the public, was already thinking about how she might reach more people and give them a greater appreciation of drama.

At home once more, Kit appeared as Mary Fitton in Clemence Dane's *Will Shakespeare,* a play that lasted only eight weeks. From that she went right into Pinero's *The Enchanted Cottage.* The play was poorly written and poorly managed, but Kit liked the role of Laura, a sort of ministering angel to her whole village.

The summer of 1923 Kit and Guthrie went on a trip to Canada where they fished, canoed, camped and swam. When they got back Kit appeared in *Casanova, The Way Things Happen,* which had only a three weeks' run, and *The Outsider* in which she played the role of a crippled girl. Audiences were tremendously moved, but an actor's strike closed the show.

After another summer in Europe Kit began rehearsals of a play called *Tiger Cats.* From the outset she disliked her role as the vain, domineering Suzanne, a detestable character. But Kit thought playing Suzanne would be good discipline. Things kept going wrong in rehearsals, including a pistol shot that burned her arm badly and Kit was miserable. Her next role as Candida in George Bernard Shaw's play by that name was much more to her liking and the press was favorable.

When Kit was assigned the role of Iris March in Michael Arlen's *The Green Hat,* directed by Guthrie, she spent hours and hours visualizing and analyzing Iris, trying to figure out how she would talk, walk, sit or use her hands. As an actress she must let Iris March, a woman hopelessly and helplessly in love, dominate her, yet she must dominate the character. Gestures and effects that were later to seem so spontaneous on the stage were painstakingly achieved. Kit played the role with great emotional intensity. At every performance of *The Green Hat* applause cascaded and the notices were excellent. One night when Kit returned to the theater she saw in blazing lights above the marquee: KATH CORNELL IN THE GREEN HAT.

"Well, Kit," said Guthrie, "it's here. Stardom. You earned it."

As a child, Katharine dreamed of such a moment, but now that it was here she found it more sobering than exciting. She hadn't really arrived. Something within was pushing and prodding her on to a greater height of perfection. The star system was wrong anyway, she thought. First and foremost was the play, and the play's message got across to the audience only if each of the cast gave his best.

After *The Green Hat* Katharine took time out to enjoy the house with which she had fallen in love. Dr. Cornell visited there frequently. To buffet suppers came Ethel Waters and George Gershwin, later entertaining other guests with music. Around the dining room table, extended to full length, sat slim, tense Noel Coward and other actors reading scripts of forthcoming plays.

After a vacation with friends in Santa Barbara, Katharine and Gertrude Macy, who was first her secretary and later a most competent manager, left for Paris to get clothes for the forthcoming role of Ellen Olenska in Edith Wharton's *The Age of Innocence*.

Both the clothes and the play were lovely, but Katharine had a bad opening night. That morning she had fallen against a chair and broken a rib, which had to be taped. Dressing for the evening performance proved to be an ordeal. Feeling weak, Katharine leaned against a pipe. The pipe was hot and she got badly burned. But in spite of a broken rib and burned arm, she gave a brilliant performance.

Kit followed *The Age of Innocence,* which got a sensational press, with *Dishonored Lady,* which was also popular. It was during a performance of this play that the audience became restless. Not knowing what might have happened, but smelling smoke, Katharine stepped out of character and with great presence of mind said calmly, "I'm sure there will be no danger if everybody leaves the house quietly. Every one of us will stand right in our places here until the house is empty."

No one left. Firemen doused the flames which had erupted in a wastebasket back of the auditorium; Katharine rang the curtain down and began the act over again.

By 1931 Katharine was well established as a star and Guthrie was a highly successful producer. They began talking about forming a company of their own. The goal, they agreed, would be to produce plays that appealed to them whether they were money-makers or not. For ten years now they had gotten along harmoniously as partners in married life with their trust and understanding of each other constantly growing; why couldn't they get along as business partners? Their enthusiasm for a script titled, *The Barretts of Wimpole Street* pushed them into final arrangements for the Cornell-McClintic Corporation.

"A bad time to experiment," friends told them when they decided to put on *The Barretts* despite the fact that twenty-seven managers had rejected it. "There's a depression; it will hit the theater hard."

Undaunted, the McClintics went ahead with their plans.
Hours on end they discussed casting, sets, lights, costumes,
entrances. Guthrie went to England to engage Brian
Aherne as Robert Browning. Katharine dug up every scrap
of information she could locate on the poetess, Elizabeth
Barrett, whose part she would play. The biggest casting
problem was getting a cocker spaniel with a good disposi-
tion for the role of Flush.

Katharine loved Elizabeth, but it was one of the most
difficult roles she ever played. There was the problem of
making her voice fill an auditorium while she was lying
in bed and supposed to sound sickly. And she felt she
wasn't doing justice to the gallant poetess. One day, worn
with anxiety, Katharine said, "I simply can't play this
part. I can't go on."

"You don't mean you can't," Guthrie answered quietly.
"You just mean that so far you never have."

The play opened in Cleveland. Except for three minutes, Katharine had to be on stage from start to finish.
The weight of her Victorian costume of brocade with three
petticoats and a wig of corkscrew curls made her perspire
profusely. But her portrayal of the ailing Elizabeth was
moving.

In New York *The Barretts* ran at the Empire Theater
for over a year—longest run of any play in history. Fan
mail poured in. Playwrights deluged Katharine with
manuscripts. Manager and movie magnates offered her
huge sums. But Katharine couldn't see herself as a screen
star.

During the fall Katharine was plagued by fatigue, eye
trouble and a drumming in the head. Doctors advised her
to take a vacation from her strenuous role as Elizabeth
Barrett. Times were bad and Katharine wanted to keep

people in the show employed, but after deciding to let the salaries go on during her absence, she took off to Bermuda for two weeks. Still unrested, she spent three days at Lake Placid walking in the country, seeing movies, reading detective stories. When she returned to New York vigorous and refreshed, *The Barretts* went on the boards again. On the last night in February, 1932, Katharine took endless curtain calls amidst flowers and tears. Outside a crowd waited in a pouring rain shouting, "Cornell! Bravo! Cornell!"

Katharine and Guthrie decided to take *The Barretts* on the road. Managers thought the idea fantastic, but Katharine felt strongly that good theater belonged to America, not just to New York. She meant to make it available. The way eager, cheering audiences packed theaters from Illinois to California justified her belief that people were hungry for the best in drama. In San Francisco the tour ended. It had been highly successful.

After a summer in Garmisch, Bavaria, Kit and Guthrie did *Lucrece,* then went into rehearsal on *Alien Corn.*

Nipped by road fever the McClintics planned another tour for the winter and spring of 1933-34. Although conscious of the problems involved in utilizing one cast of characters for three plays, they decided on *The Barretts, Candida,* and *Romeo and Juliet.* Trying Shakespeare was a bold experiment. *Romeo and Juliet* did not fare very well, but the other two plays were unqualified successes.

In Milwaukee, Minneapolis, and other northern cities the company hit snow and sub-freezing temperatures. Then as their train headed west and into Washington there was dismal and interminable rain. With Christmas Eve only hours away the cast stared disconsolately out of the windows. Katharine and Gertrude Macy, with cooperation from the steward, got up a party in the diner. After dinner the cast exchanged ten-cent gifts and sang carols. For Katharine there was something especially lovely about that Christmas Eve.

The train had been due in Seattle at 8 A.M., but a washout delayed it. That evening as the train inched over a makeshift trestle, Katharine and the others were discouraged and disappointed. Seattle was Guthrie's home town, and the Christmas night show was to have been something special—now they wouldn't even get to give it. When they finally arrived in Seattle at 11:15 P.M. they were surprised to learn from the manager that the audience was waiting for them. Weariness forgotten, they rushed to the theater. To entertain the audience they raised the curtain and let them in on the details of the stage setting. The play finally began at 1 A.M. It was an inspiring performance. Three hours later, the crowd gave the cast curtain call after curtain call.

As the tour progressed there were many amusing incidents and some that were disturbing. A performance of *Romeo and Juliet* in Oakland was punctuated by cheers and pistol shots coming from a gymnasium adjacent to the theater. The wind during a dust storm in Amarillo, Texas, made so much noise actors could hardly get their cues, and a huge concert hall served as a dressing room. In Dallas, Denver, Oklahoma City, Emporia, Omaha and Memphis people came in droves. At a lunch wagon in Montgomery, Katharine got behind the counter and cooked.

In Princeton she had a visit with the great scientist, Albert Einstein, and in Buffalo she saw her father. The tour ended in Brooklyn. The company had been on the road since November twenty-ninth, had given two hundred and twenty-five performances in seventy-five towns and played to half a million people.

In the face of blizzards, floods, poorly equipped theaters with makeshift dressing rooms and performances punctuated by wind and pistol shots, Katharine Cornell had proved herself to be a great trouper, well able to make the best of bad situations. Looking back on the rugged schedules of those hectic months with interviews and press pictures sandwiched in between rehearsals and performances, Katharine said, "I loved it. I guess I'm just a born hobo."

The success of the tour taken in the pit of the depression assured skeptical producers that the people of the whole country, not just Broadway, would support live theater.

Guthrie, dissatisfied with *Romeo and Juliet,* set to work revising the interpretation. He altered costumes, devised new effects in lighting, introduced street crowds and got Paul Nordoff to compose new music. Eliminating stilted pauses, Guthrie speeded up the tempo of the whole play.

Playing in *Saint Joan, The Wingless Victory* and the revised *Romeo and Juliet,* Katharine scored new successes. On *Romeo and Juliet* critics commented, "One of the most beautiful, most spirited, best acted Shakespearean productions of our time."

Awards which had started coming Katharine's way in the early 1930's went on and on. The University of Buffalo conferred the Chancellor's Medal upon her. Other schools—the University of Pennsylvania, the University of Wisconsin and Princeton University—followed suit with honorary degrees. For her role as Juliet, Katharine received the New York Drama League Award. She won an art citation from the National Conference of Christians and Jews, and in 1937 she was selected by Chi Omega national sorority for their award which is made annually to an American woman whose achievements are considered worthy of honor.

The night of the award banquet, Kit's hands became icy and all her old shyness rose to haunt her. After being introduced by Eleanor Roosevelt as "A woman and an artist who has done much to bring a realization of art to the people," Katharine rose shakily to give the short acceptance speech she had so carefully prepared.

Suddenly she realized she had forgotten the words. What she said was "I . . . I . . . nothing has ever happened to me that has been quite so moving." Mrs. Roosevelt put an arm around Katharine and quickly brought the meeting to a close.

In the spring of 1937 Katharine and Guthrie began to plan a round-the-world tour. The project was postponed when word came in October that Katharine's publicity manager Ray Henderson had been trapped and drowned in a seaplane in the Mediterranean. Katharine's demanding career had left little time for friends, but she was intensely loyal to the few she had, and Ray was one of them.

A steady loss of vitality and a feeling of being at cross-purposes with herself made Katharine decide to take a vacation from the theater. In her summer home, Chip-Chop, at Martha's Vineyard, she would have time to think and sort out her values. So she retreated to the low, rambling house with weathered shingles and airy, spacious rooms. She puttered around refurbishing antique furniture, worked at her weaving, cooked excellent meals and went to market in blue denim slacks. Although she bypassed parties, she was neighborly, taking time out to chat and exchange recipes. She spent long hours in the sun, swimming, supervising barbecues, playing tennis, gathering driftwood, working in her garden. Along the lonely beach she walked her highly prized dachshunds. She read mystery stories, listened to music on the radio. Occasionally she attended a movie or a baseball game where she was a vociferous fan.

It was while Katharine was at Chip-Chop that Ruth Woodbury Sedgwick persuaded her to record for her the details of her life in *I Wanted to be an Actress,* which Katharine thought should be titled *Twenty Years of Hard Work.* The book contains much that would be valuable to any girl interested in the theater. Too often would-be actresses picture Broadway as a place of stardom, lights and glamour, but it can be a street of desperation and heartbreak as well. There are always more job-seekers than jobs, and one who seeks should be very sure he has talent. Miss Cornell points out that a flair for publicity does not necessarily mean a flair for acting.

A few succeed almost overnight, but the majority, like Katharine Cornell, have come up the hard way—studied, hounded agencies, auditioned, scrounged for costumes, endured disappointments. Miss Cornell does not discount the possibility of breaks, but emphasizes that to find them in New York one has to keep tramping from one manager's office to another. Furthermore, when a break comes the chance will have been wasted unless there has been thorough preparation. For that reason Miss Cornell urges girls to get acting experience in high school, college or community plays or operettas, in drama schools or on radio. Stock show training is invaluable. Although companies like Jessie Bonstelle's, in which Katharine Cornell got her start, are now practically non-existent, there are many good summer stock theaters affording excellent opportunites.

Miss Cornell stresses the importance of a cultural background. Girls who aspire to be actresses should be familiar with the best art, the finest music, the greatest books. They should read drama columns and trade papers, study plays and acting techniques, and get acquainted with the living stage—top balcony seats never cost very much.

Because acting is strenuous, good health is a necessity. Voice is important, but voice includes diction, modulation, pitch—all of which can be improved through study. Katharine found reading French aloud was a big help. Fast memorization is an asset.

Applause and approval are only a small part of being an actress. At times the work will seem unglamorous, exhausting, disappointing. That is why Miss Cornell warns, "There should be a deep conviction that acting is the thing you must do . . . Always stay, stand the gaff and hope, as long as there is any hope, that you can bring the thing off."

Again and again Miss Cornell speaks of the necessity for willingness to take direction and to discipline one's self. In her estimation it is not beauty, eccentricity, temperament or even talent that makes an actress—it is character, self-mastery, uniqueness. And, "You can't become important unless you know how to work with people. Back of any stardom worthy of the name there is maturity and a long stage experience. Even a star cannot sit back and rest on her laurels. Always she must be studying, finding new and more perfect ways of making characterizations vital and convincing."

Katharine Cornell's months at Chip-Chop away from the theater had been a time of seeking these more perfect ways. With renewed zest she returned to her career, but the disturbed conditions in Europe made any thought of a world tour out of the question.

In 1939 Katharine went on the road with *No Time for Comedy*. She followed that with *The Doctor's Dilemma*. It was during this play that Katharine tried an experiment —a five-cent matinee for children. Her purpose was to stimulate interest in good drama at an early age. The response exceeded her rosiest expectations. *The Doctor's Dilemma* was still playing when the United States became involved in World War II.

Suddenly plays seemed unimportant. The thought uppermost in Katharine's mind was, How can I best serve my country?

She found generous uses for her time and talent. Although she had a deep dislike for microphones and had consistently refused radio contracts, she went on the air with *The Barretts* for a Red Cross benefit.

Assembling an all-star cast, Katharine and fellow actors gave thirty-five performances of *Candida* to swell the Army and Navy Relief Funds. Later she played *The Barretts* to enraptured soldier and sailor audiences at home and abroad. She was credited with helping keep morale high, but members of the armed forces helped her morale, too. Playing for these audiences she counted as among the greatest moments of her life. In addition, she and other well-known women in the theater put in untold hours making sandwiches, washing dishes, handing out doughnuts at the Stage Door Canteen. Katharine made her movie debut when it was decided activities of the canteen would be filmed to raise money for war relief.

After World War II ended, Katharine went right on surpassing herself each season. In 1955 she played the part of the gracious and gallant Countess Rosmarin in Christopher Fry's *The Dark is Light Enough,* dominating the play with a performance rich in meaning. Of all the roles she has ever played this was perhaps Katharine's favorite, mainly because of the appealing character and philosophy of the Countess. "The world does need an awful lot of things Fry says . . . We need to hear of faith and hope . . . and the triumph of the human spirit!"

Katharine Cornell was one of the last of the important actresses to agree to appear on television. The fact that in one evening she could play to more people than could be reached in two thousand performances helped win her over. In April 1956, on the twenty-fifth anniversary of its Broadway opening, Miss Cornell appeared in *The Barretts of Wimpole Street.* Although the role was old she allowed herself four weeks to adjust to a new medium which required toning down gestures and facial expressions.

Whether on stage or television, critics have described Katharine Cornell as "Gorgeous . . . regal . . . touched by the wand of genius . . . supreme in womanliness."

What brought triumph to the long-legged child who felt so unsure of herself?

Katharine herself says, "Hard work more than anything else. And the fact that the feel of it was born in me." Then there has been her genius fused with excellent health and vitality and a beautifully modulated voice charged with sincerity. But one of the most important factors has been the tenacity with which she held to her dream, despite misgivings and discouragements.

Probably there were other young actresses making the same round of casting offices as Katharine who had as much talent as she had. But they let the rebuffs, the hard work, the failures, discourage them too soon. Recovering from her early setbacks, Katharine persisted with faith and

[133]

courage. Nor did she stop with small successes. Today, after thirty-five years of acting, her face lights up when she speaks about the future. "Neither the need nor the crusade has ended for me," she says with steadfast determination, brushing aside rumors that she might be planning retirement.

Self-discipline has played an important part in Katharine's success. She has disciplined her body, her voice, her thoughts, her emotions. Actresses, she believes, have no excuse for eccentric habits or indulgence in tantrums. Katharine has great emotional intensity, but it is controlled and directed. In her relationship with others she is both understanding and kind, never holding herself aloof or guarding her talent jealously. Autograph seekers and young actresses seeking advice have received courteous consideration.

She has not depended on tricks to achieve glamour. Although she is scrupulously neat, she wears little makeup and no jewelry. Stage costumes are often elaborate, but in private life she prefers simple, crisp, beautifully tailored garments. Asked for the secret of her beauty she replied, "I have no secret. There is beauty in all people. Having found it, be true to it in thought and action."

It is this plus quality, even more than her acting technique, that has enabled her to play her roles with convincing brilliance. Intelligence linked to sensitivity, honesty and a sweetness of spirit give her a special glow. Whether the character is young or old, radiant or dull, splendid or drab, there is a uniqueness and magnetism about Katharine Cornell's acting. The seven hundredth performance has as much freshness as the first.

Then there has been her great sense of responsibility that made her take *The Barretts* on tour, play at army camps, give five-cent matinees for children. This sense of

responsibility shows up even in small details like punctuality.

Despite her devotion to drama, Katharine has never
neglected her home life. Guthrie describes their marriage
as the "they lived happily ever after" type.

As actress, actress-manager and champion of living
drama for the masses, Katharine Cornell has had a distinguished career. She cared enough for the vision that stirred
in her heart to earn it. Hers is a voice that will echo
forever through the story of the American theater.

An alert-looking girl with tousled hair and an athletic stride walked rapidly down a street in residential Chicago. Under one arm she carried a Hyde Park high school annual. When she reached home she burst into the living room where her mother sat sewing and flipped the annual open to a picture with the caption, "Girl in Brown Who Walks Alone."

"Why don't people like me?" the girl asked bitterly.

"They do like you, Amelia," her mother said. "But they don't understand you."

A shadow clouded Amelia's gray-blue eyes. "Then I'm different?" she asked.

Mrs. Earhart looked lovingly at her daughter's sensitive face. "Yes," she answered hesitantly. "But the ones who do things on their own often do the greatest things. You'll have to choose whether you'll be like others or whether you'll be yourself."

Amelia Earhart's choice to be herself, coupled with her passion to pilot planes, led her into the accomplishment of great air-borne deeds. Today with travel by air so commonplace it is hard to realize that even as recently as the thirties daily passenger flights were regarded as impractical. Only through the courage and research of skyblazers like Amelia Earhart has the Air Age been made possible.

First woman to fly the Atlantic and Pacific Oceans, she also scored an impressive number of other firsts in aviation.

Going places was a habit with the Earhart family. To be close to Amelia's father, who was an attorney and railroad agent for the Rock Island Railroad, the family either moved every few months or went along with him. Amelia loved the way their private car whisked by the white horses she and her elder sister Muriel always counted, but she wished the trains would go even faster.

Wherever they lived Amelia and Muriel found plenty of excitement. Action-loving, curious, imaginative, they spent very little time in ruffled dresses demurely playing dolls. They preferred to skate, swim, play tennis or basketball. Because the girls wore gym bloomers to play in, the neighbors thought them very daring and bold. The sisters were ardent collectors and usually had on hand a weird assortment of colored pebbles, frog eggs, toads and butterflies. Worm races with each girl prodding her entry into greater speed were a favorite pastime.

Throughout childhood Amelia displayed originality, courage and independence of spirit. Once, because she and Muriel wanted a roller coaster, they rounded up several cousins, then lugged wood, hammered and sawed, and built a rickety wooden track from the woodshed to the ground. The car was a board with roller skate wheels. Although Amelia was youngest, she was first to volunteer to ride down the rickety track. "I flew," she shouted gleefully after her first crash landing.

A further test of pluck came one day when Amelia was coasting down an icy hillside. A junkman's wagon moved along the road into the path of the sled. Amelia couldn't stop the sled, and since she knew the junkman was too deaf to hear, it would do no good to yell at him. Calmly she steered the sled so it shot between the front and hind feet of the horse, saving both the horse and herself from injury.

Another time some boys had teased the Earharts' usually good-natured dog James Ferocious until he was in a rage and pursued his tormentors, who hastily scrambled to safety. Thwarted, the big shaggy dog turned and charged madly toward Amelia.

"Run," screamed the boys.

Amelia stood her ground. "Lie down, James Ferocious," she said sternly. The dog obeyed.

At intervals, to keep the girls from having to change schools so often, the Earharts sent Amelia and Muriel to live with Grandma and Grandfather Otis in Atchison, Kansas. The big yard, with shady elms, phlox, a pair of stone dogs, and an iron deer was an interesting place, but best of all was the barn. From the seat of an old carriage the girls lashed imaginary horses to escape outlaws, enraged buffaloes or bloodthirsty savages. "The Indians will scalp us," Amelia, whose vivid imagination worked overtime, would shriek realistically.

On wintry evenings the girls used to sit in front of the fireplace reading Dickens, Thackeray or Scott, with their grandfather, a Lutheran minister, who also taught at Midland College located just outside of Atchison. The girls took their reading seriously. After finishing *Black Beauty,* they became so aroused about preventing cruelty to horses that they went around unhooking check reins every chance they got.

Summers, Amelia and Muriel joined their parents. One of Amelia's happiest vacations was spent in Minnesota where she fished with her father, swam and had a lively

Indian pony named Prince to ride. Every day she made Prince a special pie. First she took a pan and covered the bottom with tender grass. Next came a layer of crushed sugar cookies topped by leaves and fragrant clover blossoms. As a finishing touch she spelled out the word Prince with mulberries.

When vacations were over Amelia returned to the classroom, sometimes in Atchison, sometimes wherever her parents happened to be. One of her favorite subjects was geography. She wanted to visit every single place the teacher pointed out on the globe. All the moving gave Amelia ease in meeting new people, but because of it she never became one of a close-knit circle of schoolgirls planning good times and sharing secrets.

The year 1911 brought sad changes to the Earhart family. Grandmother Otis died and the Atchison home was sold. Because of poor health Mr. Earhart resigned from his position with the railroad and settled in St. Paul, Minnesota. But then the Earharts moved once more—this time to Chicago. Amelia, now searching for scientific truths, felt she didn't fit very well among girls at Hyde Park School, whose chief interests seemed to be boys, clothes and a good time.

After graduation from Hyde Park she enrolled in the Ogontz School near Philadelphia. As the United States became more and more involved in World War I, Amelia became increasingly restless. During Christmas vacation on a visit to her sister Muriel, who was attending school in Toronto, Canada, Amelia was deeply concerned over the number of wounded soldiers she kept seeing on the streets. Upon her return home Amelia broached the idea of hospital work.

"That means giving up graduating," said Mrs. Earhart.

Amelia didn't care. Instead of serving in an American hospital she returned to Toronto where she served as a nurses' aide at Spadina Military Hospital in Toronto.

Most of her off-duty moments were spent watching war-scarred planes flown by pilots training for overseas service. There was nothing she wanted more than she wanted to fly, but she couldn't get permission to go up.

At the end of the war Amelia returned to the United States. Since aviation seemed closed to women, she decided to enroll for a course in auto mechanics in Northampton. Later, still seeking an outlet for her scientific bent, she enrolled for a pre-medical course at Columbia University. She also signed up for courses at Barnard. At Columbia she often did many things that startled her classmates, such as climbing into the lap of a statue in front of the library to do her studying. Although she did good work at Columbia, Amelia decided she wasn't the right type of person to be a doctor.

Withdrawing from the university, she went to live with her parents who had moved to California. The Earhart home was located fairly close to an airfield. Amelia was fascinated by the planes overhead, and after attending an air meet, she felt she simply couldn't stand it not to fly. One day she took money intended for a dress and boarded a streetcar to Rogers Airport. Walking over to a pilot who was tinkering on a little, red, two-seated plane with an open cockpit, she said, "I want to go up."

The pilot grinned. "Okay," he said. "I'm Frank Hawks." The plane jounced over uneven ground, then roared into the air, flying above green hills, oil derricks and cars looking no bigger than toys. Amelia's heart soared with the plane. She loved the speed, the altitude, the freedom—the something more than that for which she had no words. There was no doubt in her mind about the future—she had to be a pilot.

Amelia's parents tried to discourage her. Almost no women flew planes, they pointed out. Flying lessons would be expensive, and then there were the risks involved—planes in the twenties were flimsily constructed and risky contraptions compared to today's sturdy ships.

To all their arguments Amelia's answer was, "I'll earn money for lessons—I'll die if I don't learn to fly."

"You'll probably die if you do," her father said grimly.

Amelia tried to forget about becoming a pilot, but every time a plane droned overheard she would relive the excitement of that flight with Frank Hawks—the beauty—that sense of being apart from man-made ugliness.

Flying would give her the freedom she so desperately needed. To get money for lessons Amelia took a job with the telephone company. Her instructor at the airfield was Neta Snook, a lively, self-reliant woman with close-cropped red hair, who wore dirty overalls and often substituted a dash of engine grease for make-up.

Anxious to look like a flyer, Amelia had her hair cut short and bought a leather jacket, which she slept in to wear off the telltale newness. Her only disappointment with her air instruction was that she had to stay grounded so much of the time studying instruments and motors. Because the lessons were expensive, learning to fly was a long-drawn-out process, but Amelia had a core of tough tenacity. The day came when she could solo. She'd never been any happier.

Mrs. Earhart helped Amelia buy a small second-hand plane. To meet her end of the payments and take care of the upkeep, Amelia worked at various jobs. She even drove a truck for a while. Then she took training in photography and got a position in a studio.

Despite limitations of time and finances, and a sinus difficulty which sapped her energy, Amelia continued her aerial activities. Flying a little open-cockpit Kinner Airster biplane, she established an altitude record for women. And in 1923 she became the first woman to win a coveted license from the Federation Aeronautique Internationale. But no job opened. Carrying mail and passengers by plane was still in the experimental stage, and for every opening there were a dozen World War I pilots.

Finally Amelia decided she'd better continue her education and plan to make her living by teaching. In the fall of 1927, after a short time at Columbia University, she went to Boston to become a resident social worker at Denison House. Although she would have preferred to be a pilot, she gave the best she had to the job at hand. She showed a genuine interest toward the pupils in her classes but she still kept her hand in aviation by joining the Boston chapter of the National Aeronautic Association.

One day while she was supervising a group of children at Denison House, a little boy came running from the office to call her to the telephone. When Amelia answered, a man's voice said, "Would you like to fly the Atlantic?"

At first Amelia thought it was some kind of joke, but she soon found out that a Mrs. Frederick Guest, a wealthy, socially prominent Englishwoman born in America, wanted to sponsor a good-will flight between the United States and England. There would be a male pilot and mechanic, but as the third member of the crew Mrs. Guest wanted a woman.

Amelia went to New York for the interview, but almost

immediately gave up all hope of being chosen. According to the men who interviewed her Mrs. Guest wanted some-one who oozed social charm, grace, beauty and education. Amelia felt she just didn't measure up. When they told her she had been selected she could hardly believe it. Not wanting to worry her family or friends, Amelia kept the proposed flight a secret. In those days the hazards of an oceanic flight were much greater than they are today.

On June 5, 1938, Amelia, pilot Bill Stultz and mechanic Louis Gordon took off in a flimsy plane called the *Friend-ship* for the small fishing village of Trepassey Bay, New-foundland. Twelve days later, after tiresome delays, the trans-oceanic flight got under way. Wedged between the extra gas tanks Amelia felt the plane rock and stagger as it soared out over the banks of silver, frothy clouds. In order to keep an eye on the instruments she crouched behind the pilot and from time to time jotted down ob-servations or radio reports from steamers.

Hours passed. Amelia had hoped to do some of the flying, but because of rain and heavy headwinds Stultz stayed at the controls. Their first mishap was having the radio go dead. Some time later Stultz said, "We've less than an hour's supply of gas."

But before the situation had become critical, Stultz set the *Friendship's* pontoons down on the gun-metal bay of Burry Point, Wales, where a boatman took them ashore. Although Amelia insisted she had done little more than keep a log and pass sandwiches, she was snowed under with telegrams, invitations, gifts. Heralded as "Lady Lindy" she attended luncheons, teas, saw a great military pageant involving the Royal Air Force, toured Bucking-ham Palace and danced with the Prince of Wales at the Embassy Club.

The English, who had half-expected to meet a massive, mannish woman, were surprised to see a graceful person with beautiful hands and unusual charm who could talk about a great deal more than engines and altimeters.

When Amelia returned to America, New Yorkers gave her a rousing welcome. A simple, sincere person, Amelia felt the credit she was receiving was false and was disturbed by the waves of publicity swirling around her. But one thing was sure—she was back in aviation to stay. She could no longer deny the innermost desire of her heart.

Amelia resigned from social service work, accepted a position as Aviation Editor of *Cosmopolitan* magazine, became Vice-President of Ludington Airlines. With diligence and concentration she worked hard at improving her flying knowledge. She got her Air Transportation License, tested an Autogiro on a long flight and made a transcontinental solo flight. After her first parachute jump she reported, "It's more fun than any roller coaster I ever rode."

Anxious to get some of her ideas about flying into words, Amelia wrote a book titled *20 Hours, 10 Minutes*. Publisher George Putnam was interested in the manuscript but wanted revisions. While working together on the final copy Amelia and George fell in love.

But Amelia, realizing the strength of her dedication to flying, felt uncertain about marriage. Fortunately, Putnam, who was a "doer" himself and was Director of the American Museum of Natural History Greenland Expedition, understood and sympathized with her aspirations. They were married in February, 1931, in the home of George's mother at Noank, Connecticut.

Amelia didn't have much of a flair for housework, but she was a gracious hostess. She and George spent many happy hours at their country home in Rye gardening, riding horseback, playing croquet on a lawn shaded by oaks and elms. Indoors they liked to read, listen to music, or sit in front of the fireplace and talk.

By 1932 Amelia had become an experienced flyer. Now she felt ready to tackle the Atlantic alone. Perhaps the only value of the flight would be to demonstrate the reliability of modern aircraft, but it certainly wouldn't be "just another stunt." George promised cooperation.

Fully aware of the hazards of her projected trip, Amelia made her preparations carefully. Day after day she tested instruments, loads, take-offs. To permit addition of extra fuel tanks on her Lockheed, she sheared off every bit of non-essential equipment. Because she wanted no ballyhoo, those who shared the plans for the flight were pledged to secrecy, including Dr. James Kimball, the coordinator of meteorological data upon which she depended for the go-ahead signal on weather.

Finally, on May 20 the expected call from Dr. Kimball came through. Amelia changed into her flying suit. Knowing that pounds, even ounces counted, she limited her luggage to a comb and toothbrush; for food she took a Thermos of soup and a can of tomato juice.

So Amelia would be fresh to start the oceanic hop, the well-known pilot Bernt Balchen flew her to Harbour Grace. Alone she winged away from the Newfoundland coast into a lingering sunset. Heading out over the giddily tossing whitecaps of the Atlantic, Amelia had the feeling she and the plane, looking like some great red insect, were one.

At first all went well. Then the altimeter failed. About 11 P.M. a storm began to jerk and toss the plane. Jagged spears of lightning stabbed the sky. When the Lockheed slowed up, Amelia knew the wings were picking up ice and she ought to descend, but without an altimeter that was dangerous.

Having no choice, she dropped down until the waves heaving underneath her were dangerously close. She tried to ignore the long miles that still lay ahead of her. Suddenly she saw an ugly tongue of red flame erupt through a broken weld on a manifold ring of the engine. Weakened metal rattled ominously. The ship seemed doomed.

As night dissolved into the pearly gray of dawn, the flames looked less menacing, but new trouble developed. One of the reserve tanks was leaking. Amelia would have to set the plane down very soon, but where? She couldn't do it on the water. And the land she kept seeing turned out to be only a mirage.

At last she did actually see green hills underneath her, but a gray curtain of rain made visibility almost zero. Circling and circling she finally landed in a pasture. It was exactly fourteen hours and fifty-six minutes since she had left Harbour Grace, a distance of two thousand and twenty-six miles.

As soon as the wheels of her plane touched the ground, an amazed farmhand came running toward her.

"I've just come over from America," Amelia explained as she climbed down from the plane.

"Do ye be tellin' me now," the farmhand spluttered.

Amelia found she had landed close to Londonderry, Ireland. The owner of the farm drove her to Londonderry to send a cablegram to George. The cablegram revealed her whereabouts.

The American ambassador invited her to be a guest at the Embassy; Lady Astor wired an invitation; King George sent congratulations. And next day Paramount News sent a plane to take her to London. Wearing borrowed clothes, Amelia went shopping for a new wardrobe.

George Putnam hurried over from America to help her bear up under the heavy schedule of banquets and awards, among which was a Certificate of Honorary Membership in the British Guild of Air Pilots and Navigators.

From England Amelia and George went to France. There Amelia was elaborately entertained and received the Cross of Knight of the Legion of Honor.

After being feted in Italy by Mussolini, she and George went on to Brussels where they were guests of the King and Queen of Belgium. The king, a big friendly man with a shock of unruly hair, had a great deal to say about aviation. After an informal lunch, the queen, using an old-fashioned, battered box camera, took snapshots of Amelia and George, and the king gave Amelia the Cross of the Chevalier of the Order of Leopold.

On June 15 Amelia and George embarked for home. Upon their arrival in New York reporters swooped down on Amelia like sparrows. A crowd numbering thousands cheered and showered her with ticker tape as she rode down Broadway. Fans mobbed her. Amelia, who never thought of herself as courageous and always insisted that in the air there were so many decisions to make that there wasn't time for fear, couldn't understand the whirl of activities in her honor. "Everyone has his own Atlantic to fly," she said modestly.

She was the first woman to receive the Distinguished Flying Cross, and on June 21, after a dinner at the White House, Amelia received the National Geographic Society's special gold medal. In presenting the medal President Hoover said in part: "Her success has not been won by the selfish pursuit of a purely personal ambition."

[147]

Amelia, who was always uncomfortable when praised publicly, accepted the medals as graciously as possible.

Tired of the spotlight of publicity, she looked forward to some uncluttered, secluded days in Rye where she could enjoy the quieter aspects of life and write about some of the ideas crowding up inside her. From the choppy but vivid notes she was always jotting down at odd intervals she did complete a book called *The Fun of It,* expressing some of her thoughts about flying.

But the seclusion she longed for never materialized. She found that fame brings restrictions and cumulative responsibilities. The telephone jangled. There were hundreds of invitations to speak, to appear at social functions. And there were avalanches of mail. Many of the letters praised her as a "gallant pioneer," but others condemned her as a "foolhardy nitwit." At first Amelia tried to answer all her mail personally, but it became an impossible burden.

Many distinguished visitors came to the house at Rye. With Admiral Byrd, Will Rogers, Auguste Piccard and the Lindberghs, the talk was mostly about flying. But when Elsa Schiaparelli came, she and Amelia had a lot to say about functional clothes for active women. Later Amelia designed a few herself.

Amelia had expected that the publicity would soon die down, but there were articles, songs, poems apostrophizing her as the woman of the ages, and innumerable news items. Not all of the press notices were favorable. Amelia's belief in her work and her unfailing sense of humor made her almost immune to attack, but when she was criticized for saying she had flown the Atlantic because she wanted to, her answer was, "To want in one's heart to do a thing for its own sake, to enjoy doing it, to concentrate all one's energies on doing it—that is not only the surest **guarantee** of its success, it is also being true to oneself."

When the Universal studio tried to persuade Amelia to come to Hollywood, her answer was, "No movies for me."

Although Amelia was not a joiner, she helped organize the Ninety-Nines, so named because there were ninety-nine members, all woman fliers, and for a time she served as president. She also belonged to the Society of Women Geographers and was awarded their gold medal. This and numerous other awards—bright ribbons, gleaming jeweled decorations from foreign governments and eminent scientific organizations—Amelia kept in a small leather suitcase. Although she appreciated them, she never paraded them.

Because she needed funds for her flying, she turned to lecturing. At first she was a diffident speaker, but soon developed a good delivery. Audiences liked her enthusiasm, charm and gracious manner. With all the dedicated zeal of a missionary she tried to popularize flying, to get people to see aviation's possibilities for passenger and mail service, for protection of international friendships. When a heckler pointed out that airplanes were not as safe as automobiles, her rejoiner was, "Ox carts are safer than autos, but people today prefer to drive autos."

In April of 1933 Amelia was a guest of President and Mrs. Roosevelt at a dinner at The White House. When in the course of the evening Mrs. Roosevelt said rather wistfully that she had never experienced a night flight, Amelia said impulsively, "Will you go with me? Now?"

"Why . . . why, yes," answered Mrs. Roosevelt. So the First Lady and the First Lady of the Air went off like two conspirators—both in white satin evening gowns.

[149]

Despite her busy life, Amelia still managed a few quiet interludes at Rye. After the place was partly destroyed by fire in 1934, she and George began planning a home in North Hollywood. Although Amelia didn't make a crusade of it, she was utterly and completely opposed to war. When Congresswoman O'Day said publicly she was a pacificist and would probably be placed in a federal penitentiary in case of war, Amelia gleefully telegraphed, "Me, too."

Ever since the Atlantic flight Amelia had toyed with the idea of a Pacific solo which she hoped might mark a little more clearly the pathway over which planes of the future would fly. Because a continent is easier to hit than an island, she chose to fly from Hawaii toward the United States.

Late one afternoon in January of 1935, Amelia, piloting a Lockheed Vega, thundered off into the sky and winged her way over twenty-four hundred miles of ocean. When she arrived in Oakland, she was so tired her knees would hardly hold her up. But the success of this flight had given her new confidence in her dream of a round-the-world trip at the equator.

Shortly after her Pacific solo, Amelia was appointed to the Bureau of Air Commerce to demonstrate the new directional air apparatus, and in April she took off for Mexico on a good-will flight. That night as she soared over the silvery dome of Mount Wilson Observatory and the white haze of the Gulf of California, she felt very close to the stars. Mountain-rimmed Mexico City greeted her with wild enthusiasm. She dined with the President of Mexico, lunched with artist Diego Rivera and received a medal from the American Geographical Society. She enjoyed the floating gardens, an exhibition game of *jai alai,* a fiesta, concerts and a May Day celebrated with fire-works. Coming home she made a nonstop flight from Mexico City to Newark, scoring another first.

The following June, Dr. Edward C. Elliot, President of Purdue University, announced that Amelia, who had become an international celebrity, had been appointed a visiting faculty member at that institution. Her official title was Adviser in Aeronautics, and she was to spend as much time at Purdue as she could spare from other duties. Purdue was one of the first universities to offer training in aeronautical engineering and aviation in its curriculum, and the equipment was better than at many commercial airports.

When she was on the campus Amelia stayed at a dormitory and the girls were thrilled at the way she fitted into their way of life. Although she was a stern self-disciplinarian and neither drank nor smoked, she was fun-loving and very approachable. Students imitated her smartly designed sports clothes and wind-blown haircut.

In the classroom Amelia was a stimulating teacher. She had great sympathy with the girls who wanted to tinker with machines and find out what made engines perk, even if they did get grease in their hair. During guidance sessions, she urged students really to find themselves, to keep searching until they found work they could believe in and contribute to. "There may not be any more geographical frontiers to cross," she told her students, "but there are plenty of them left in the world of politics, economics, science and the arts."

When speaking specifically of aviation, Amelia stressed the necessity for a girl to have intelligence, perseverance, poise and a genuine enthusiasm for flying. To be a pilot, a mechanical bent and physical fitness, including twenty-

twenty vision, are essentials, but Amelia gave equal emphasis to courage, alertness, steady nerves, sound judgment and emotional stability. Although today the hazards of aviation have greatly diminished, these same qualities are still requisites for girls who aspire to fly.

Amelia warned that to break into this field, essentially a man's world, would take real competence. The opportunities in 1935 were, of course, more limited than they are today. Now women have gained a toehold in almost every phase of aviation.

There are openings for minor executives, traffic control operators, personnel workers, aerial photographers, meteorologists, mechanics, teletype operators, hostesses, line crewmen, librarians, clerks, ticket or passenger agents. Some airports and aviation schools not only welcome, but actually prefer, women as flight instructors, because of their greater patience. There are ten thousand women in military aviation service. But although there are close to twelve thousand licensed women pilots, openings for them in commercial lines are still extremely limited.

The educational requirements Amelia outlined for her classes at Purdue remain much the same. However, as planes become more complex, more knowledge is necessary. Subjects most frequently mentioned in the curriculums of aviation schools are algebra, geometry (both solid and plane, trigonometry, physics, chemistry, mechanical drawing, a foreign language, geography, economics, psychology, blueprint reading. Flight training includes studying innumerable details pertaining to navigation—wind, speed, altitude, landing gear; reading and controling various instruments, indicators, gauges, knobs, switches. Civil air regulations must also be mastered. The

[152]

training is intensive, requiring great willingness to work and study, and the courses are expensive.

In her teaching Amelia managed to get across many of her own ideas about life. "There's a difference between a daydream and a real desire that gets hold of the heart," she told her students. "Young people are too timid about trying Atlantics."

There were some who criticized Amelia's work at Purdue, charging that she was luring girls away from marriage into careers. But the officials were so impressed by her work that in the summer of 1936 they presented her with an all metal Lockheed Electra equipped with every instrument then known to aviation. Amelia was delighted with the speed and performance of her flying laboratory. She felt an obligation to come up with some constructive accomplishments.

For a long time she had felt there had been too much concentration on the mechanical aspects of flying—too little on the human element. Her clear, inquiring mind sought answers to questions such as the effects of altitude, air pressure, fatigue and diet on those who flew.

Now that she had a plane that would take her farther and faster than any plane she had previously owned, Amelia decided to do the technical experimentation she'd been wanting to do, a flight around the world at the equator, she felt would give "added knowledge of flying, and of people, and of myself." Preparations were more intensive than for the Atlantic or Pacific solo. She spent hours digesting mechanical information and poring over maps that to her always seemed like the start of an adventure. At night, lying in bed, she reviewed possible emergencies. What would you do if . . . To insure safety the answers must be autonomic. A lover of accuracy, Amelia was strict and methodical in her preparations. She studied terrains and climates; planned emergency landing possibilities, fuel caches, and airport services; rounded up special landing permits and had extra parts shipped to airports.

Amelia's first globe-girdling attempt in 1937 was a failure. She got as far as Honolulu, but the morning she was taking off from the Luke Field Runway, something went wrong. There was a crunching, grinding sound of twisting metal. Sparks flew up. "Fire!" cried panicky spectators. The landing gear was stripped, the right wheel sheared off, but the *Electra* didn't explode, and Amelia, who with cool courage had cut the switches, emerged unscathed. She stood staring dismally at the beautiful shining Electra tilted on one side like a battered bird with a broken wing.

"Will you try again?" a reporter asked Amelia.

"Of course," she told him.

Shortly afterward she got a wire from George, who was in Oakland: WHETHER YOU WANT TO CALL IT A DAY OR KEEP ON GOING LATER IS EQUALLY JAKE WITH ME.

The wrecked Electra was brought back to Burbank, California for lengthy repairs. At that point it would have been easy to scuttle her plans, but giving up was not Amelia's nature. She still felt a responsibility to produce some practical results.

Because of the delay and the change in weather, she decided it would be best to make her second start from the East Coast. On June 1 Amelia and George stood hand in hand in the dim chill of the hangar building at the Miami airport waiting for mechanics to do some final work on the Electra. Seeing the shadow of concern on George's face, Amelia would have canceled the flight if he had said the word, but knowing what the trip meant to her, he couldn't hold her back, especially since she had pledged that this would be her last long record-making flight.

Just as the sun was pushing aside the grayness of dawn, Amelia, looking very small, climbed into the cockpit of the big ship. She waved good-by to the crowd that had gathered, then with her navigator, Lieutenant Commander Fred Noonan, she revved up the motor and taxied to the end of the runway. The Electra rose smoothly into the Florida dawn and disappeared into the immensity of space reaching out beyond any known frontiers.

The Electra winged over aquamarine water, over islands to Puerto Rico, Venezuela, to Senegal in French West Africa. In Dakar, Amelia marveled at the intense colors, strong smells, mountains of peanuts in the markets and tall black figures in headdresses. Lunching with the Governor General, she tried to remember her French, but kept coming up with useless phrases such as, "my aunt's umbrella."

Amelia and Noonan flew on over land that from the air reminded them of papier-mâché relief maps with deserts, mirrored seas, and dwarf mountains. Everywhere they landed Amelia found oil drums with her name on them and a competent crew to service the Electra. In Karachi, India, she had a long-distance call from her husband and rode a camel. In her notes she wrote—"The camel unhinged himself in extraordinary fashion. Camels should have shock absorbers."

From Karachi, Amelia and Noonan skimmed over mountains with backs like sharks, through monsoons, above rice paddies.

In notes sent back to her husband, Amelia mentioned the gleaming white buildings of Calcutta, rickshaws of

Singapore, pagodas and singsong prayers. After landing in Lae, New Guinea, she wrote George, "The whole world has passed behind except this ocean." She also spoke about being homesick.

The morning they were to leave Lae, Amelia appeared on the jungle-cleared landing field wearing slacks and a plaid shirt. Slim, agile, her tawny short hair rumpled and damp from a drizzle, she looked younger than her thirty-nine years. Anxiously she scanned the black clouds bulking up in the east and thought of their next goal. Howland Island, she had been told, was a coral reef less than two miles long, completely uninhabited. If the Electra flew into a storm, it would be easy to overshoot that fleck of coral which lay over 2,556 miles away, surrounded by a vast expanse of water. But Amelia was eager to be off. Before she joined Noonan in the plane, she turned and smilingly waved good-by to the Dutch officials and natives who had gathered to bid them farewell.

As the Electra neared the vicinity of Howland Island, the *Itasca,* a Coast Guard cutter which had been previously alerted to keep contact, picked up a message from the Electra.

There were several exchanges between the cutter and the plane, but the abrupt, only partly intelligible phrases from the Electra indicated serious trouble.

Then in a high-pitched, anxious voice the message came from the Electra, "We must be on you but cannot see you. Gas running low."

The captain of the *Itasca* ordered the men to stoke the boilers, sending up billows of black smoke.

Then another message came from the Electra—"We are receiving your signals, but are unable to get a minimum (bearing) . Go ahead with signals."

Despite frantic signals nothing more was heard from the Electra. When the news came on Saturday, July 3, 1937, that America's most famous woman flyer was missing, the nation was stunned. But there was still hope. Amelia had stared down disaster at other times. After all, the Electra had been equipped with signal kit, rubber lifeboat and life jackets, and the largest sea hunt in history had been launched. The aircraft carrier *U.S.S. Lexington* steamed over the rolling seas to join the search, but a freak sleet storm hampered the search.

While rumors swept round the world, the hunt went on for months, even in uncharted islands, but neither land nor sea yielded any trace of the missing flyers. Amelia Earhart, who had lived for flying, had died for it.

In point of fact the Amelia Earhart story ended when George Putnam released a letter written to him and marked to be read only if she did not return: "Please know that I am quite aware of the hazards," it read. "I want to do it because I want to do it. . . . Women must try to do things men have tried. When they fail, their failure must be but a challenge to others."

The kind of woman Amelia was showed through in her attitude toward flying. She wanted to do everything possible, to awaken people to the potentials of the air age, but money, the clamor of the crowd, rewards as such, meant almost nothing to her.

"The fun of it" was one of her favorite expressions. Whether teaching, writing, or flying, she enjoyed the work and gave herself to it whole-heartedly, always directing her energy purposefully. An expert in human relations, Amelia saw good in everyone. She was as much at ease with royalty as with the mechanics who serviced her planes. Her smile and good-natured matter-of-factness made even strangers her well-wishers. To her, adventure wasn't going places—it was a state of mind.

Amelia loved beauty. In the book *Last Flight,* based on Amelia's notes and published by George Putnam, she spoke of cloud shadows "like giant flowers dark on the green sea, of curving moons, snow-capped peaks and saffron deserts."

Emotionally mature, Amelia remained calm, poised and good-humored in difficult situations. She had a striking integrity. Throughout her life she acted and thought with originality and a willingness to stake her life on what she felt was worth doing. "Courage is the price that life exacts for granting peace," she once said. Never lacking in courage, Amelia Earhart became a blazer of skyway trails—trails that are shrinking the distances between nations and people. Aloft in limitless space, companioned by wind and stars, she also found peace.

# 7: ELEANOR ROOSEVELT

## Citizen of the World

When Eleanor Roosevelt was five years old the family went to Europe. On a sightseeing trip to Sorrento, Italy, her father rented a donkey. Astride the small, big-eared animal, Eleanor rode off happily with a bare-footed boy as guide. Her father was surprised later to see them returning with the guide riding the mule. "What happened?" he asked.

"My guide cut his foot," explained Eleanor. "I made him ride."

In later life the same kind of concern for others, linked with a relentless energy, set her off on a campaign for social justice that made her an international celebrity. Columnist, lecturer, globe-trotter, once first lady of the land, Eleanor Roosevelt was also the first woman United States Representative to the General Assembly of the United Nations.

She was born October 11, 1884, in New York City. Her father, a wealthy, personable and charming man, was the younger brother of Theodore Roosevelt. Eleanor's mother came from an equally impressive and wealthy family noted for distinguished appearance and social grace and descended from Philip Livingston, a signer of the Declaration of Independence.

Childhood was a time of frustration and unhappiness

for Eleanor. Although her eyes were lovely and her hair beautiful, she had protruding teeth and a plainness that made her feel like an ugly duckling compared with her beautiful mother. Her self-conscious shyness became all the more painful when her mother, with no thought of wounding her, sometimes called her Granny because she was so serious and old-fashioned. Quite often she failed to do what her mother considered "proper," and got the idea she'd never be able to do what her mother expected.

It seemed to Eleanor that her mother spent most of her time caring for a younger brother Elliott, who was called Ellie, or going off to teas and parties. The child was grateful when her mother read to her or let her touch her jewels when she was dressing to go out. But Eleanor's craving for attention and admiration went unsatisfied. The only moments when she felt wanted and useful came when her mother had headaches and let Eleanor stroke her hair.

With her father, to whom she was devoted, Eleanor could forget her shyness. But under the strain of business and social activities Mr. Roosevelt became ill, and for long periods at a time he would be in some sanitorium where Eleanor was not permitted to visit him. To her loneliness for her father was added worry about what might be wrong with him.

Then when Eleanor was five there was the European trip, when she and her father set forth on delightful adventures. In Venice they boated down canals, with her father singing like a gondolier. On a visit to Mt. Vesuvius they tossed pennies into a crater and got them back lava-coated.

But the good times ended when Mr. Roosevelt again entered a sanitorium and Eleanor was placed in a French convent. Because she was an English-speaking foreigner and a Protestant, the other little girls considered her an outsider and never invited her to join in their games.

While they were in Paris, Eleanor's baby brother Hall was born, and shortly afterward Mrs. Roosevelt took the three children back to America. At home a governess was engaged to teach them, but even with a governess Eleanor was often too timid to recite, although she might know her lesson perfectly.

Eleanor was only eight when her mother died of diphtheria. Her maternal grandmother, Mrs. Valentine G. Hall, took the three youngsters into her fashionable but somber New York home on West Thirty-Seventh street. Mr. Roosevelt came for the funeral but left shortly afterwards. "Write to me, and study hard," he told Eleanor. "Be a good girl and grow into a woman I'll be proud of."

Eleanor tried, but her life seemed one continuous struggle for self-improvement. She had to wear braces to correct a curvature of the spine, braces to straighten her teeth. Grandmother Hall was a strict disciplinarian and was constantly at Eleanor to improve her skills or manners. There were endless Bible verses to be learned in French, and rules and rules to be obeyed. "It's lots easier for Grandmother to say no than it is for her to say yes," Eleanor told Ellie.

Grandmother Hall insisted that Eleanor wear flannel underwear, long black stockings, and high-laced shoes. The dresses she bought for the long-legged, awkward child were inappropriate for her height. Thinking that ballet would give Eleanor grace, Grandmother Hall arranged for dancing lessons. Although Eleanor enjoyed the lessons, she never became like the willowy girls she envied in class.

Lonely for her father, sensitive to criticism, ashamed of her awkwardness, Eleanor retreated more and more into herself. The death of her brother Ellie, the same winter she lost her mother, increased her loneliness. On the few occasions when she was with other children, aside from her brother Hall, Eleanor found herself poorly prepared for their sports and light-hearted fun. She was tortured by the feeling that she was odd or different.

Despite her own unhappiness, or perhaps because of it, Eleanor was very sympathetic toward the needs of others. When her Uncle Vallie took her along to help with the Christmas tree in Hell's Kitchen in New York City, she was shocked by what she saw in this slum area. Young as she was, she felt she must do something for these people in torn and faded clothing.

She was just as touched by a visit to crippled children at Orthopedic Hospital and she tried to comfort the tiny patients by showing them the brace she wore. "See all I can do with it," she told them.

Living at Grandmother Hall's had some bright spots. Eleanor loved to read, and her late grandfather's library kept her well supplied with books. She especially liked the ones that pictured life in other countries and left her longing to visit these far-away places.

Two young aunts and two uncles who also lived at Grandmother Hall's frequently thought up interesting and exciting things to do. Aunt Pussie took Eleanor to the theater and to concerts. Although Eleanor had little talent as a performer, she loved music.

The best days of Eleanor's childhood were when her father came. At the sound of his voice she would slide down the bannisters and catapult into his arms. Always he had a delightful surprise for her—a toy, a pet, a ride in a high dog cart. But these happy, carefree days ended when Eleanor was nine. After her father's death she took refuge in a dream world in which she pretended she and her father were doing things together.

Summers spent at Grandmother Hall's estate at Oak Terrace on the Hudson River helped Eleanor forget her grief. There she had a playhouse in the woods, a bicycle and a pony to ride. And she loved the horses and dogs— especially a dog named Mickey that looked like a polar bear. Until they were caught she and her brother Hall found it amusing to climb out an upstairs window and walk around on the gutter to a window on the opposite side of the house.

Eleanor rejoiced in the companionship the estate afforded—picnics, games, sometimes a girl her own age who came to play, good times with the servants. Occasionally the laundress took her to her home, where Eleanor ate German food and picked apples. Only Sundays were dull. Then there were no games, no books except religious ones and Eleanor was expected to teach hymns, collects and catechisms to the coachman's little daughter.

Eleanor's greatest trial at Oak Terrace was sewing. If a darn or a mend didn't suit her governess, the woman snipped it out, leaving a still larger hole.

About once a summer Eleanor visited at her Uncle Teddy's great gabled house called Sagamore Hill on Long Island Sound. With her cousins, whooping with delight, she would slide, roll, tumble at a dizzy pace down Cooper's Bluff, a sandy incline sloping sharply to the beach. When the children tired of swimming, riding horseback, rowing a boat, they would gather around Uncle Teddy, who told exciting stories of cowboys, cattle thieves, grizzly bears and Indians. In the telling he hammered home the necessity for courage and moral stamina.

In Eleanor's early teens the highlight of the year was

always a Christmas party at Auntie Corrine's (Mrs. Douglas Robinson), although this was partly painful because Eleanor stood in awe of her sophisticated cousin Alice. There was, however, one great satisfaction—Cousin Franklin gave most of his attention to her.

When she was fifteen, Eleanor entered Allenswood school in England. Here she was subjected to a rigid schedule: There were morning walks after breakfast—often taken in a chilling fog, rooms had to be kept in perfect order, and the food, eaten to the accompaniment of French conversation, was unappetizing. Eleanor especially disliked the clammy suet puddings.

But she enjoyed her classes with Mlle. Souvestre, headmistress of the school, a vivid and entertaining person. While at the school, Eleanor, who had never excelled at sports, became a very good hockey player and for the first time in her life she had the feeling of really belonging to a group.

During school vacations Eleanor visited friends or relatives in England or on the continent, or traveled with Mlle. Souvestre. The wise and understanding headmistress, wanting to foster Eleanor's self-reliance, assigned her such responsiiblties as ticket buying. Under her teacher's guidance, Eleanor developed a deep appreciation of nature and of the customs of different people. She learned to find beauty in every form—in the colored sail of a fishing boat or a cathedral spire in moonlight.

After three happy years at Allenswood Eleanor wanted to stay on for a fourth, but her grandmother ordered her home. "Eighteen," she insisted, "is the age for coming out."

Grandmother Hall placed Eleanor's name on all the right lists. At dinners, dances, parties, the tall, shy girl, unaware of her attractive features—sparking blue eyes, a sweet smile, interesting hands—felt herself something of a wallflower.

Rebelling at the rigidity of being with the so-called right people, attending endless parties, reading only certain prescribed books, Eleanor began taking on projects. She helped the Consumer's League investigate working conditions in factories and taught calisthenics and dancing at a settlement house. She took almost complete responsibility for her young brother Hall, and enrolled him at Groton.

Becoming better acquainted with her gay, self-confident cousin Franklin, who made it easy for her to talk about things they were both interested in—literature, history, foreign lands—Eleanor fell in love. But Franklin's mother disapproved of Eleanor as a future wife for her son and hustled him off on a cruise to the West Indies, hoping he would change his mind.

During a visit with her Aunt Bye in Washington, D. C., plenty of eligible escorts surrounded Eleanor, but none interested her as much as Franklin. In her battle against sensitivity Aunt Bye was a big help. "Just be sure you would not be ashamed to explain your actions to someone you love, and do what seems right," she told Eleanor.

The cruise didn't change Franklin's mind. Shortly after he returned, the engagement was announced. Together the lovers saw their Uncle Teddy inaugurated as President of the United States.

For the wedding on March 17, 1905, Eleanor wore a heavy satin dress with shirred tulle in the neck and long sleeves. The bride received less attention than Uncle Teddy.

Because Franklin was still in Law School at Columbia

University, the real honeymoon was put off until summer. Then the happy couple went to Europe where they attended the theater in Paris, motored through the Alps, floated down Venetian canals, rode across the moors of Scotland.

During the early years of her married life, Eleanor had to make many difficult adjustments. Strict and methodical in her habits, she often found it hard to go along with Franklin's easy-going ways, although they were in agreement on basic values. Living in the home of Franklin's headstrong and domineering mother, who had rigid ideas on how things should be done, restricted Eleanor's freedom and intensified her struggle with a sense of personal inadequacy.

The birth of baby Anna on May 3, 1906, brought new responsibilities. Anna was followed by James and Elliott. Franklin Delano, Junior, born in 1909, died when only a few months old.

When Franklin was elected a state senator in New York, Eleanor moved to Albany reluctantly, dreading public life. But she had been trained to do what she ought to do, not what she wanted to do and, feeling it was her duty to be interested in her husband's work, she frequently sat in the visitors' gallery at the state legislature. Impelled to do something about problems she heard discussed, she tried to get women interested in campaigns and elections.

In the spring of 1913 Franklin was appointed Assistant Secretary of the Navy. This meant living in Washington where Eleanor could run her own household. Still shy, she was a little awed by the people in whose orbit Franklin's work drew her, but she was very conscientious in her duties as a government official's wife. As she gave of her energy and interest, she developed poise and new understanding of the world around her. The political scene fascinated her, but she felt her first duty was to the children. The family spent many evenings listening to music, reading aloud or just talking. Speaking of that period of her life Eleanor says, "I wish now I could have taught them more wisdom somehow—saved them more heartaches and mistakes."

A second child named Franklin was born in 1914, John in 1916. When the United States became involved in World War I Eleanor did Red Cross work, served as hostess at a canteen, visited the wounded in hospitals.

In the summer of 1921 the family vacationed at their summer home on Campobello Island, New Brunswick, Canada. When a forest fire broke out Franklin volunteered as a firefighter. After the fire was under control he came home and took a swim. Later he complained of chills and fatigue. Before he could be gotten to a hospital paralysis had set in.

"Infantile paralysis," the doctors told Eleanor. "He'll be in a wheelchair the rest of his life."

Franklin's mother and his friends took this to mean that his political career was at an end, but his doctor and Eleanor would not have it that way. To help keep Franklin's name before the public she embarked on a series of speeches, although her shyness made public appearances an ordeal. She invited political leaders to come in for conferences with her husband, became finance chairman of the New York Democratic State Committee and took a position teaching history and literature several days a week at the Todhunter School for Girls.

When Franklin went to Warm Springs, Georgia, for treatment, Eleanor realized that the children were going to miss his compansionship. Trying to make up some of the loss, she learned to swim so she could supervise the children in the water. She rode horseback with the youngsters, and took them on camping trips.

Shuttling back and forth between New York and Warm Springs, Eleanor encouraged Franklin to greater physical, mental and political achievements. By 1928 he could walk with the aid of a cane. After he became Governor of New York, Eleanor helped whenever possible.

Franklin's election as President of the United States in 1932 left Eleanor both elated and sad. She knew how much it would change their personal lives.

On the eve of the inauguration young Democrats were singing "Happy Days are Here Again," but the occasion was far from a light-hearted one for the Roosevelts. They were conscious of an America plunged into depression. Right in Washington there were breadlines, soup kitchens, men sleeping on park benches. Soberly, the Roosevelts moved to the White House, taking Anna and her two children with them. At the time Elliott and James were both married, Franklin and John in college.

Eleanor found it hard to remember she was the wife of the President and often did not conform to tradition. She startled the household staff by helping rearrange furniture and running the elevator herself. At the first few parties she forgot that none of the guests could leave until she left. The White House itself both surprised and shocked Eleanor. She hadn't known that, although wages of the staff were paid by the federal government, food bills came out of the presidential salary. She was surprised at the little economies—mended rugs, darned tablecloths—and shocked by the kitchen infested with rats and cockroaches.

Mail, even with the help of secretaries, was a big problem. Almost fanatical about answering letters, Eleanor never permitted a secretary to sign her name for her. Some of those who wrote complimented Eleanor, but many criticized her activities or those of her family, her taste in hats, dust on a White House railing or the condition of squirrels on the lawn. Some of the letters carried appeals for help and it was often hard to tell whether the need was genuine or just a hoax, as was the case with a girl who wrote that she was valedictorian of her class but had nothing to wear for graduation except coveralls. Would Mrs. Roosevelt send a dress of specified size and color? Investigation showed the girl wasn't valedictorian—in fact she wasn't even graduating.

People wrote asking for everything from autographs or demitasse cups to an apron made from the president's shirt tail to be sold at a bazaar.

At first Eleanor resented all the stuffy formalities pertaining to White House social life. Protocol, she thought, should be left to the State Department. All one needed to do at a reception or dinner was to be sure that there was enough food and act glad to see those who were invited. She soon discovered that the rules solved such ticklish problems as who should be seated next to whom.

Eleanor liked meeting new people, but she preferred small groups to the hundreds who came to big teas or receptions. But although her feet might be aching, her head whirling, guests saw only a poised, dignified woman who received everyone with gracious friendliness. Quick to recognize the needs of others, tactful and enthusiastic, Eleanor developed a knack for letting people know she had a personal interest in them. Worried visitors to the White House were soon put at ease. Placed in a situation where in a single year thousands of people came for tea and hundreds were dinner or house guests, she learned to take even the big receptions in stride. For these occasions she dressed magnificently, often wearing a white gown with a diamond necklace.

When a woman asked Eleanor, "What do you notice in a reception line—hats, dresses?" Eleanor answered, "Faces. I think What a pretty face, What a kind face."

Eleanor's daily schedules at the White House were very strenuous. Mornings usually began with an early horseback ride or a swim. After breakfast she made plans with her housekeeper. Were there enough sandwiches for a tea for two hundred? What should they serve when the Premier of France arrived? Then followed a conference with her social secretaries, Edith Helm and Malvina Thompson. The rest of the day might include a luncheon, speech, press conference—in fact, anything from a tour of the White House with visiting lobstermen to a train trip to New York to investigate factory conditions. Riding the train, Eleanor was likely to read a pamphlet on a bill before Congress, jot down a few notes for a book review or knit.

The usual routines were stepped up to an even more hectic pace when important personages from abroad visited the White House. The entertainment of the King and Queen of England in 1939 included everything from hot dogs at Hyde Park to musicales and stately pageantry.

What disturbed Eleanor most about being the wife of the President was the feeling of living in a goldfish bowl. The Roosevelts had been in the White House only three months when marital difficulties thrust Elliott into the spotlight. Normal family life seemed an impossibility. One night one of the boys returned home from a dance in a ramshackle car with no identification. He had trouble convincing a guard on duty that he was a Roosevelt. "What kind of place is this, anyway?" he asked his parents the next morning, "where you can't get into your own home?"

Eleanor tried to make the White House more homelike by moving out some of the fragile furniture and replacing it with substantial pieces more suited to her burly sons. Occasionally the family got together informally to scramble eggs on a Sunday night. There would be noisy excitement when Eleanor impersonated a ferocious lion for her grandchildren. But such festivities were infrequent.

It was even hard to keep special holidays intact. The children and grandchildren usually managed to get to the White House for stocking hanging, tree trimming, and the reading of *A Christmas Carol*. But there were many interrupting obligations—gifts and parties for the clerical staff, household staff and Secret Service; attendance at the Community Christmas Tree; assistance at the National Theater party for underprivileged children; distribution of Salvation Army baskets.

Despite their background of wealth both the Roosevelts understood the effects of poverty and believed government had a responsibility toward the jobless. Eleanor's efforts in behalf of improved working conditions began at the White House, where she provided better facilities for the household staff.

To get a more complete picture of the effects of the economic depression sweeping the country, trouble-shooter Eleanor inspected coal mines, factories, work camps. Critics attacked her as a snoopy do-gooder, but she learned not to be indignant at caricatures and distorted stories about "Madame Gadabout," and laughed as much as anyone over a cartoon of two miners looking down a shaft, then at each other. "Why, there's Eleanor Roosevelt!" one of them exclaimed.

The miserable effects of the depression on the mining towns, factory and farm areas shocked and saddened Eleanor. When she took the problems of these people to the President, he listened. He respected her opinion, not just because she was his wife, but because he knew she did her own thinking. When governmental relief came through slowly, Eleanor often sponsored projects on her own.

One of these was establishment of two places in New York where unemployed girls could get hot lunches, have a place to rest and repair their clothes. She helped get jobs for unemployed teachers and set up a W.P.A. school to train household help. It was she who protested the waste in destroying surplus crops and suggested that the food be given to people on relief.

When the bonus marchers descended on Washington in 1933, Eleanor, genuinely interested in their problems, went to their camp, although she had been warned that the men were in an ugly mood. Her short speech was cordially received; and as she drove away, cries of "Good luck!" followed her.

Eleanor won support for her job-creating ideas for young people, including the National Youth Administration and the Civilian Conservation Corps Camps, established April 5, 1933 to provide a combination of manual and mental opportunities for young men without jobs. The N.Y.A. supplemented the work of the C.C.C. by offering projects to help high school and college youngsters finish school. She gave friendly counseling and guidance to many young people whose plans for education, jobs, marriage were upset by the depression.

One day an unshaven, disheveled young man walked up to her car in a gas station and asked for some money. Eleanor gave him ten dollars and asked him to come see her to discuss getting work.

"You'll never see the money or the young man again," a friend predicted gloomily.

But the young man showed up later, scrubbed and shaven. Eleanor got him a job in a State Park. He later repaid the money.

A champion of underprivileged minorities, whether social, racial or religious, Eleanor fought to improve school and hospital facilities for Negroes. When the Daughters of the American Revolution refused the use of Constitution Hall to Marian Anderson, Eleanor resigned from the organization. She promoted labor legislation, sponsored activities of Girl Scouts and Camp Fire Girls.

The wide range of Eleanor's activities brought some friendly spoofing at a stunt night staged by newspaper women and wives of the Gridiron Club:

Little Boy Blue, come blow your horn,
The sheep's in the meadow, the cow's in the corn.
But thinking of fences, and speaking of sheep,
When, if ever, does Eleanor sleep?

Eleanor always read the President's speeches, sometimes making a contribution to them. She also penciled out confidential memos. Keen, astute in her understanding of the country's needs, she was really a minister without portfolio. More impatient than Franklin, she was always wanting things to happen. "Let's do something," she would say. "If we don't do what I suggest, all right, but let's do *something*."

During her first years at the White House, Eleanor had refused to discuss political issues, fearing that they might be construed as opinions of her husband. But after some coaching from Louis Howe, newspaperman and personal secretary who became a confidential advisor, and who urged her to go out and speak, she walked right into the teeth of public controversy. In case of differences of opinion on issues, Franklin encouraged her to go ahead and state her own views.

In 1940 there was a split in the Democratic Convention. The Party Chairman asked Eleanor to fly to Chicago. In the hot, thronged stadium she found an unruly, hostile convention. Quietly, but firmly, Eleanor called for unity. "The emergency," she said, "is too great to permit party jealousy." Her conviction won support of the convention.

When the United States entered World War II after the attack on Pearl Harbor, Eleanor's expression of sympathy for the Japanese being herded into internment camps brought criticism swirling about her. Undaunted, she shuttled back and forth across the country appraising the state of the nation and promoting civil defense.

To obtain better understanding of a wartime ally, the President sent her to England. A guest of the King and Queen at Buckingham Palace, Eleanor found window-panes broken by bombing, replaced by isinglass. The palace was cold, the food plain and uninteresting. Visiting military bases, shipyards, factories, air raid shelters and bombed-out areas, Eleanor marveled at the people's ability to carry on.

Back home she watched as eagerly as any mother for letters from James, Elliott, Franklin Jr., and John, who were overseas. Although the boys made exceptional military records there were charges that they were shown favoritism. Ignoring the sniping and the uncomplimentary name calling directed at her—"suitcase wife," "freeloader" —Eleanor visited the w.a.c. at Des Moines, inspected war plants in Mexico and aircraft factories in Canada.

Her hardest assignment came when the President asked her to make a tour of the Pacific. She flew or sailed over mine-infested seas to visit hospitals, rest camps, recreation centers. Keeping up a machine-gun pace, she got up before 6 a.m. to eat with enlisted men and to watch jungle warfare. On besieged islands she spoke to huge audiences. "She did more for our morale than a dozen u.s.o. shows," G.I.'s said of her.

Thinner by thirty pounds and more tired than she had ever been in her life, Eleanor came home bringing hundreds of addresses of relatives of boys in service to call upon or to write to. About the trip she said, "I wished I could be changed in some magic way into the mother or sweetheart, wife or sister these men longed to see."

In March of 1944, Eleanor made a similar tour to the Caribbean area, visiting fly-infested huts in Puerto Rico. Back at the White House she had to cope with a never-ending stream of visitors—royal refugees, celebrities, Prime Ministers on wartime missions, aid-seekers like Madame Chiang Kai-shek.

Because of duties in Washington, Mrs. Roosevelt stayed behind when the President, in April 1945, went to Warm Springs, Georgia, for a rest. There he was taken ill.

A short time later a call from the White House came to Eleanor while she was attending a benefit. Her heart froze. She was almost certain what the message would be. Even in her grief over her husband's death, Eleanor's thoughts reached out to people who, having lost their leader in the midst of a critical stage of the war, were anxious and disturbed.

She had no definite plans for the future, but it was with relief that she moved out of the White House where she had lived for twelve years under the pitiless searchlight of public opinion.

Behind her Eleanor left a trail of shattered traditions. She had almost completely changed the citizen's idea of what the president's wife should be. Refusing round-the-clock secret service surveillance, she had driven her own car or traveled on buses and planes chatting with fellow passengers, workers, housewives. The White House had become a more friendly place, where a duke and a farmer might sit down at the same table to eat corned beef.

Feeling people had a right to know what was going on, Eleanor had inaugurated the custom of strictly feminine news conferences. Treating the women of the press as people whose good judgment and loyalty could be trusted, she answered questions frankly and good-humoredly.

As is customary for the wives of ex-presidents, Eleanor disappeared from the public scene. Much of her time was spent at Val-Kill cottage at Hyde Park, where she was surrounded by books, flowers, snapshots of her family. In her library she did a great deal of writing—books, articles, newspaper columns similar to "My Day," which she started in the White House with the idea of showing people what life was like there.

Of those difficult, fatiguing years, Eleanor wrote in her book *This I Remember:* "It was almost as if I had erected someone a little outside of myself who was the President's wife. I was lost somewhere deep down inside myself."

For a time she enjoyed the quiet existence. Then the

old tempest of energy began once more to rage within her. She disliked bridge and grew tired of concerts, the theater, lectures. More and more she began to realize she had a destiny of her own to fulfill. And there were causes she wanted to promote—especially world peace.

Vigorously she undertook a colossal daily schedule which often left her doing two things at once, but doing them to the best of her ability. With the help of a secretary she answered the staggering piles of mail which continued to come her way. Especially interested in the queries of girls wanting to know about the world of politics, she gave detailed advice. Any girl interested in politics as a career should be active in school organizations, acquire an understanding of government and laws from local to international level and learn at least one foreign language. She should read newspapers and news magazines, listen to newscasts, try to see the shades of opinion represented, but form her own opinions. Ability to speak fluently and clearly is invaluable, and any girl who expects to enter politics should get all the experience possible in making public appearances. She should learn to meet people easily and understand them. Working with the political party in her community, ringing doorbells at election time, stuffing envelopes, poll watching all give excellent experience. Politics is no place for the weak of heart, but a fertile field for any intelligent girl who has the courage to stand for her convictions even in the face of pressure or defeat.

Speaking on such themes as "I believe peace is something you must cultivate with great care and tenderness," Eleanor went on the air. Thanks to speech lessons, her once high, somewhat squeaky voice had become warm and pleasant. Noting that she was always ready to accept criticism and turn it to self-improvement, a radio technician said of her, "She's a honey."

Eleanor's voice traveled to France in the French tongue, to Spain in the Spanish tongue. She lectured on many platforms both at home and abroad and served on the Board of Trustees of Brandeis University.

When Eleanor received word she had been appointed to serve as United States representative to the General Assembly of the United Nations, she felt she had no background for such an assignment. As the only woman on the United States delegation for the meeting of the General Assembly in London, she felt unwelcome and conducted herself with cautious shyness. The first time she had to speak in argument with Russia's Vishinsky, she felt tense and excited.

Heart and soul in the work, she soon astonished everyone by her grasp of world affairs. Outspoken, straightforward, she gave opinions that were both fearless and wise. If she became involved in a debate in which bitter statements were made, she saw them as a difference of opinion and not a personal attack on her; and so, even when others around her became ruffled or angry, she remained poised and serene. With brilliance and energetic drive she concerned herself with refugees, world health, equality. A great idealist, but also a doer, she served capably as Chairman of the Human Rights Commission, cutting red tape to a minimum. Accused of being too idealistic, she answered, "Remember that every step forward is the product of someone who dreamed dreams."

On a trip to India Eleanor maintained a pace which brought assistants practically to the verge of collapse. She spoke to the Indian parliament, visited mud huts and tenements, talked to veiled women, taught teen-agers to dance the Sir Roger de Coverly. On a scorching hot day in Bombay, thousands of people milled about in front of the hotel where Eleanor was staying. When she came out to a waiting automobile they shouted, "Eleanor Roosevelt, *zindabad!*" (Long live Eleanor Roosevelt.) Before entering the car, Eleanor bowed her head and pressed her palms together in the Hindu posture of friendship. Flattered that she had taken the trouble to learn a respected custom, the crowd went wild.

With the endurance of a circus trouper, Eleanor went on to Singapore and other Far Eastern cities.

In January of 1953, after seven years in the United Nations where she had become one of the most popular members, Eleanor resigned. At the end of the General Assembly meeting in Paris, she took the long way home, visiting Israel and Lebanon, where the government furnished her a car and military escort.

Back at Hyde Park Eleanor spent much time out-of-doors, swimming daily and taking long walks. Wearing a seersucker dress and trailed by her black Scottie, "Mr. Duffie," she looked much like a country grandmother as she gathered pansies, picked raspberries or staged picnics for guests ranging from her grandchildren to the Emperor of Ethiopia.

But her other routines were far from grandmotherly. She continued to attend meetings, lecture, appear on radio and television, write, and cope with tall stacks of mail. Wise but not old, alert and interested, she went right on working for the American Association for the United Nations. "If you abandon faith in the world, what's the use of living?" she asks those who say the United Nations is a failure.

Already a seasoned traveler, she logged up additional

mileage via jeep, ricksha, oxcart, plane, train or bus. In Japan she spoke at many meetings on the meaning of democracy. On a Russian trip she interviewed various officials including Khrushchev at his summer home in Yalta. "The present generation of adults in Russia is just what the leaders in the Kremlin ordered," she concluded after observing the hundreds of ways in which people have been conditioned to do certain things in certain situations.

At home and abroad honors have continued to come Eleanor's way. Many institutions of higher learning, including England's famous Oxford University, have conferred degrees upon Eleanor Roosevelt. Her picture has appeared upon the stamps of Lebanon and El Salvador. In polls she has run far ahead of any other woman in the esteem of the public, whether in Birmingham or Bombay.

Mrs. Roosevelt's success can be partly explained by her amazing energy. Even today she can wear younger people to a frazzle. The only part of her anatomy which ever gives her trouble are her feet, affected by so much standing at receptions, which she laughingly refers to as "White House feet."

As basic to her success as her energy was Eleanor Roosevelt's early acceptance of the belief that life requires tremendous self-discipline. She also learned that the way to conquer the self-indulgence of shyness is to have outgoing interests. Goodness, just simple goodness, is the quality which most impresses those who know her. A reporter who went to Hyde Park on a muggy day to cover details of one of her numerous parties for underprivileged boys found her looking hot but cheerful as she buttered dozens of hot dog rolls.

"Why butter them?" he queried. "The boys will eat them anyway."

"When the King and Queen of England had hot dogs here we buttered the rolls," she replied. "Why should I do less for the boys from Wiltwick?"

If it were not for her fantastic generosity Mrs. Roosevelt would be rich. Recipients of gifts from her personal fortune range from the crippled boy who longed for a guitar to the American Friends Service Committee, which in one year alone received seventy-two thousand dollars. Because of Eleanor Roosevelt's interest in people of all races, religions, creeds, women are a little closer to equality, workers are less likely to be exploited and Negroes have won a little more recognition. Columnist Westbrook Pegler, often her severest critic, once conceded, "There is no other who works as hard or knows the low-down truth about peoples and the troubles in their hearts as she does."

A society girl who found social life boring, born to wealth but with a deep concern for the poor, Eleanor Roosevelt has become a defender of human rights, friend of the forgotten, citizen of the world. Her influence on her times has seldom been equaled by any other woman.

## 8: KATE SMITH

### Pioneer of the Air-waves

From childhood Kate Smith's greatest desire was to sing. Even before she had learned to read she would stand in church and carol lustily from an upside-down hymn book. The stained glass windows, flowers, or sermon meant little to her, but the boom and roll of the organ, the hymns and anthems made her shivery with excitement. In the years that followed, Kate kept right on singing no matter what the obstacles. Addition of her second interest—people—only inspired her to become a better musician. Because Kate Smith genuinely wanted to sing and serve she became an outstanding pioneer in the field of radio entertainment, a woman beloved by thousands of listeners.

Her name is Kathryn Elizabeth. Born on May Day 1909 in Greenville, Virginia, she was only a year old when the family moved to Washington, D. C. Kate sang as naturally as a lark, but she also got encouragement from her father, a news dealer who had a fine tenor voice. And her mother, a good pianist, helped out by playing her accompaniments.

By the time she was five, Kate was singing at Sunday School pageants and church suppers. During World War I she made the rounds of army camps close to Washington and on one occasion President Wilson was in the audience. But appearing before the president excited the scrawny, long-legged eight-year-old Kate less than singing for the

Blue Devils—a hundred French soldiers sent to this country to help promote Liberty Loan rallies. When Mrs. Smith and Kate, her taffy-colored pigtails tied in blue satin bows, arrived at Peck Memorial Chapel where the program for the Blue Devils was to be given, they found a big, shoving crowd. Kate's only worry was that her white dress might get crumpled or her black patent leather slippers stepped on. As soon as she walked out onto the platform she was captivated by the handsome French soldiers wearing light blue uniforms, jaunty caps and a lot of medals on their chests. Her singing of *Over There* was followed by applause, shouts and requests. In the end everybody sang. When the last note had died away the captain of the Blue Devils stepped to the platform. He gave Kate a kiss on the cheek and popped a Blue Devil cap on her head. Carried away by enthusiasm for the French soldiers she marched to the Union Station with them to wave farewell. By the time Mrs. Smith caught up with her, Kate's white dress was soiled, her shoes scuffed, one blue ribbon bow untied, but the Blue Devil cap sat cockily on her head.

At the end of World War I, General Pershing pinned a medal on Kate for her help in maintaining military morale. "Keep on singing, child," he told her. Kate did. Once at school when her teacher had a sore throat, Kate taught the music class for two weeks.

But she also found plenty of time to be a normal child. With her sister Helene she climbed trees, played rough-and-ready games, raced after fire engines. The summer Kate was nine, the Smiths vacationed at Colonial Beach, Virginia. One day Kate and a playmate took to the water with a canoe. Neither of the girls was very adept at handling it. When clouds bulked up in the sky threatening a storm, they paddled frantically toward shore. The combination of big waves and their own unskilled effort caused the canoe to capsize. Kate swam a few frenzied strokes, grabbed the canoe, then kicked free and tried to swim again. When they were finally rescued by a man in a launch, she said, "You didn't have to come after me. Can't you see that I can swim?" Next morning, having gained rather than lost confidence because of her ducking, Kate began to improve steadily in her swimming technique.

All her life Kate has wanted to do things for other people in a great big way. If she had a birthday party she insisted on inviting everyone in her grade. And the birthday cake had to be an oversized one with thick frosting.

When Kate was fourteen a thyroid condition caused her to put on an alarming number of pounds. Getting clothes that were big enough became a problem, but an even greater problem was her sensitivity to what people had to say about her weight. At school, classmates laughed at her and never seemed to tire of wisecracks and gags. Kate loved sports and group activities, but gave them up rather than take the constant ribbing. By-passing huddles of girls chattering about homework, parties, dates, boys, she headed for home the minute school was out. There she would shut herself up in her room for hours at a time to think black, hopeless thoughts. When she tried to diet she only made herself sick.

"Forget your handicap," her grandmother advised. "Concentrate on your voice."

Kate tried, but when she sang she felt as if everyone must be looking at her, instead of listening. Fat or not, she was determined to go on singing. She took advantage of every musical opportunity that came her way—church choirs, amateur theatricals, parties, local benefit shows.

After learning the tricky steps of the Charleston, she often combined dancing with a song for her last number. She won numerous contests and many a five-dollar gold piece.

These successes made Kate decide she wanted to go into show business. That was not a popular suggestion. Nobody in the Smith family had ever been on the stage. It wasn't the right choice for a carefully reared girl, they argued. And anyway, who ever heard of anyone as large as she was making a go in the entertainment world? Because of family pressure, Kate registered for a nursing course at George Washington Hospital. Being able to help people was fine, but she disliked studying chemistry and bacteriology. The hospital routines and smells, the sickness that seemed to hang in the air like a fog, depressed her. And it was hard to walk about in rubber-soled shoes and talk in hushed tones when what she wanted to do was lift her voice in song. Finally Kate persuaded her parents that her heart was in singing, not in nursing.

Kate continued to appear on local talent and benefit shows, winning some applause and recognition. One night when a performer at Keith's vaudeville house failed to show up, she was asked to fill in. This led to a role as Tiny Little in the musical comedy *Honeymoon Lane*. Kate was still in her teens and the family objected to having her go off to New York. But once Kate convinced them she had to sing and that this was her big chance, they helped her with preparations.

Through the long and torrid summer days, Kate danced in rehearsals until she was ready to drop, and she sang until she thought her voice would wear out. Nights, completely exhausted, she lay on her bed in a small, stuffy room in an obscure hotel, homesick for friends and family. Nobody in this strange, heartless city cared what happened to her, she thought gloomily. Night after night hot tears of loneliness splashed over her rumpled pillow. Kate would have given up, but she couldn't quit singing. And at the time job openings were far from plentiful.

Before the New York run, *Honeymoon Lane* opened for a try-out at Atlantic City on August 29, 1926. Excited by the footlights, the audiences, the applause, Kate found the stage a great adventure and temporarily forgot homesickness. She was even more elated and confident when her act began stopping the show. Then in September *Honeymoon Lane* opened in New York. The flowers and telegrams from home made Kate feel like a seasoned trouper. She didn't even suffer any stage fright. This was the career she had dreamed, planned and slaved for, she thought jubilantly, moving about in a rosy glow.

But the glow faded when Kate saw the papers next morning. Complimentary comments by the critics were tinged by sarcasm—"Kate is immense in more ways than one." They virtually overlooked her voice, her dancing technique.

No matter how hard Kate worked at developing her voice, audiences seemed much more interested in her antics as a fat girl. Two years after her debut in *Honeymoon Lane* she got a role as a Negro mammy in the show *Hit the Deck*. Blackened with burnt cork she stopped the show practically every night, singing a syncopated spiritual, "Hallelujah." But again it became apparent that as far as New Yorkers were concerned, her singing was only secondary. Kate was disappointed and discouraged, but comforted herself with the thought that at least she was learning a lot.

Then quite unexpectedly she got a part in *Flying High,* co-starring with Bert Lahr. Here was a real triumph at last, she told herself happily. Imagine starring on Broadway! The night the show opened she dashed gaily out on the stage in a flaming red costume.

Almost immediately the rowdy jokes began about her food habits, her size, her shape. To the deeply humiliated Kate the laughter of the audience sounded unfriendly. She tried to forget her weight, but being surrounded by slender chorines didn't help. Neither did the audience—they applauded her singing, but they never missed a chance to laugh. As the show went on, her pounds weighed heavily, but her heart was heavier still. She hadn't expected to be treated as a clown. Some day she'd make audiences appreciate the quality of her singing, she thought bitterly. But night after night the same thing happened. Kate became more ashamed, embarrassed and discouraged. On-stage she sometimes flushed with anger. Off-stage, tears came as she removed her make-up.

During her free time she was more miserable and lonely than she had ever been in her whole life. Kate got a few invitations to supper parties and night clubs, but night clubs bored her. She neither smoked nor drank, and she didn't meet the kind of people who had been her friends at home. Occasionally her mother came for a week-end, but the relief was only temporary. Then her first real sorrow came with the loss of her father.

Many times Kate felt she should quit the show and go home. But she stuck it out in the hope things would get better.

They got worse. A telegram from her grandparents with the news that they were coming to see her on stage threw Kate into a panic. She loved her grandparents devotedly, but they were old-fashioned and deeply religious, and she could imagine what their reactions would be to the show's humor. In desperation Kate concocted wild schemes to head them off. But she couldn't be dishonest enough to pretend sickness. Apprehensively she awaited their arrival.

When she spotted her grandparents in the theater, Kate groaned inwardly. Later, in the hotel, the three had a long talk. "No amount of money," said Grandmother, "can pay you for going through all that." Kate didn't really want to stay with the show—the money she earned didn't make up for the way she smarted under the ridicule. But she couldn't face giving up. Somehow she had to find a way to keep on singing.

Her grandparents left without her. The show became a hit, but Kate took little pleasure in it. One night a note came to Kate's dressing room from a Ted Collins. Probably a playboy, she thought dismally. Kate was about to refuse to see him when the words "Important business" on the back of the card caught her eye.

"I'll see him for five minutes," she told the stage door man.

Ted Collins, a man with keen, dark eyes and a quick smile, explained that he was scouting talent for Columbia recordings, although he had come to this particular show only because he had missed a train. "You ought to be making records instead of letting comedians stick darts in you," Ted told her.

Kate felt an immediate confidence in this quick-witted, capable young man who didn't treat her like an oversized comedienne. When she told him a little about her disappointments and unhappiness with show business, he listened sympathetically and offered to have recordings made of her voice. Kate would have liked to quit the show then and there, but felt she shouldn't go back on her word. Ten minutes later the two had reached an agreement. Kate would finish the season with *Flying High,* but meanwhile she'd start recording.

In the days that followed, Ted became a good friend and counselor. He made Kate's life more bearable by getting others in the show to let up on their ribbing, but the real partnership between them was launched the afternoon Ted said, "I'll be your manager from now on. All you have to do is sing."

When her stint with *Flying High* had ended, Kate went home for a rest and a vacation. It ended abruptly. Ted summoned her to New York for an engagement at the Capitol Theater. Here Kate got to sing some of the tunes she liked—sweet, tender songs like "Danny Boy."

Ted believed Kate had a future and started to groom her for radio. Under his coaching, she gained self-confidence and security—the hurt she had carried around inside began to heal. She learned to brush off barbed remarks about her weight, even to joke about it. As she became less concerned about her appearance she found that other people seemed to notice it less.

In the spring of 1931 Kate's initial broadcast for the Columbia Broadcasting System was scheduled. As she stood waiting for the "on the air" signal, she became very nervous. What if her voice failed? What if listeners didn't like her singing? Then the comforting thought came to her that her mother would be listening, and she certainly approved of Kate's singing. Maybe there were others like her sitting at their radios. For them Kate could give her best. When the signal came she sang naturally and confidently. "Swell!" Ted told her when she had finished. Congratulations telephoned by her mother a short time later gave Kate all the assurance she needed.

At first Kate was on the air with only two fifteen-minute spots weekly at 11:30 P.M. When she worried about the time and the program, Ted told her, "You sing. I'll fight the battles." Kate's next assignment was almost as bad. She was on daily, and at an earlier hour, but in competition with the popular *Amos n' Andy* show.

Kate waited anxiously for the fan mail to come in. Her voice was not a great one, but letters and telegrams pouring in from Maine to California proved that she was singing songs people wanted to hear in a way they liked.

By fall, having won a reputation as "Songbird of the South," Kate got a daily half-hour program at a better time and a four-figure monthly salary. For a theme song she used, "When the Moon Comes Over the Mountain." Keeping her radio programs fresh and original meant long, strenuous hours of rehearsing and planning, but Kate loved the work. On each program she tried to have one popular song, one tune on the romantic side and a memory song—one recalling a happy moment of long ago. Frequently she included a classic, an operatic aria or a standard favorite such as "The Last Rose of Summer."

Because she wanted to put on a neighborly, friendly kind of program, Kate tried to visualize families who might be sitting and listening in. Her "Hello, everybody," was sincere, her "Thanks for listenin'" spoken in all humility.

In 1932 Kate went to Hollywood to appear in the movie, *Hello, Everybody*. To her, Hollywood and everything in it seemed high-powered and super-colossal. Ill-at-ease and overwhelmed by the necessity for wearing orchids and diamonds and acting like a celebrity, Kate took to her bed for three days. But once on her feet again she mustered her usual zest for work. She reported in at the studio about eight o'clock in the morning and stayed on the job until late afternoon. Except for the discomfort of heat from the klieg lights she found the procedures interesting. In the lunchroom she saw actors and actresses with garbs varying from Puritan women and Catholic priests to gamblers and cowboys. The Paramount set, a little city in itself, was quite fascinating, although Kate often smiled at such incongruities as a façade of Notre Dame cathedral only yards away from a faked Swiss chalet. She especially liked the days when filming was done on the Lasky Ranch and a picnic spirit prevailed.

People were wonderful to Kate, but she didn't have the feeling of belonging in Hollywood. Late hours never suited her; sophisticated talk bored her. Even at a big dinner given at the Coconut Grove in her honor she was mentally looking for an exit almost before the complimentary speeches had been concluded. The more Kate saw of insincerity, artificiality and string-pulling, the more she disliked the place. As Christmas approached she became homesick for snow, snappy weather, and most of all for her family. The day was saved by the arrival of her mother and sister Helene. At Agua Caliente they swam in the warm blue water of the Pacific. Other highlights were visits to Catalina Island, Palm Springs and Lake Arrowhead.

In 1933 Kate and Ted got road fever. They pulled together a troupe of forty, calling themselves *The Swanee Review*. It was really a variety show with rope twirling, dancing, comedy and songs. Kate had planned to leave the broadcasting studio for only a few weeks but, although America was deep in a depression, one engagement led to another. It was over eight months before Kate returned to New York.

The Swanee Review traveled in two private cars. For Kate, keeping the show on the road meant catching trains at midnight in drafty stations, sleeping in strange hotels, eating at outlandish hours, getting into a black dress sparkling with sequins to sing and dance the Charleston four or five times a day. After a performance on stage, Kate, dripping with perspiration, would have a shower and massage and then rest, read or write postcards home until time for the next show. But she loved show business. The glamour lay not in footlights or headlines, but in the comradeship of fellow troupers and in the way audiences greeted her as if they already knew her. Everywhere the troupe journeyed—Buffalo, Akron, Chicago, Detroit—they found friends. Crowds came to the train bringing gifts and flowers. Mayors gave luncheons. In Minneapolis Kate went sleigh riding. In Sioux City, Iowa, the Winnebago tribe of Sioux Indians gave her the name *Hom'-o-goo-winga,* meaning Glory of The Moon.

A Memphis admirer gave Kate a wobbly-legged fox terrier nicknamed Snoonie. The terrier wriggled his way into the hearts of the troupe, also made a nuisance of himself barking, getting loose, in hotels, chewing up Kate's slippers and powder puffs. Once he ventured out on the stage during the show, but the applause frightened him. Snoonie soon had the company of a white Spitz, a tawny fat Chow and a sparrow with a broken wing. The sparrow, christened Chirpy, lived in a grass-lined shoe box in Kate's dressing room where she fed him lavishly on birdseed, lettuce and crumbs. After Chirpy's wing mended, Kate released him in open country dotted by Texas bluebonnets.

In San Antonio the troupe sampled frijoles, tamales, golf courses and Texan hospitality. They also acquired a baby goat dubbed Pinky. When Pinky seemed lonely and wouldn't eat, Pedro, Pinky's brother, was brought in. But Pinky and Pedro didn't take well to show business. Their bleating became a problem and one afternoon while Kate was holding a high note in a sentimental song, there was a long-drawn-out chorus of *ma-a-a's* off-stage. The following day Pinky and Pedro left the show.

While Kate was in Dallas, Governor "Ma" Ferguson made her a Texas ranger and presented her with a gun, badge, spurs and ten-gallon hat.

From El Paso the show headed for Tucson, where the thermometer stood at a hundred and ten degrees. By auto they traveled to Phoenix across desert made colorful by flowering cacti and flaming sunsets, and then entrained for Los Angeles. Shows on the West Coast were interspersed with swimming and deep-sea fishing in the Pacific, sightseeing in Chinatown and a drive along the Columbia River.

The tour ended in Seattle. Instead of relief, Kate felt a wrench as she and Ted Collins and his wife prepared for a vacation in the Canadian Rockies. Forgetting the discomforts, hard work, and erratic schedules, she remembered the happy experiences of sharing and giving pleasure.

Kate's radio fans welcomed her return to the air waves and she soon gained immense popularity. To the public her rise to fame looked like a series of lucky breaks. Unlike most musicians, Kate did not spend years and years taking voice lessons. Born with a sense of pitch so perfect that a band leader once sent her a pitch pipe asking her to test it for accuracy, Kate had no trouble singing in tune. She had an inborn sense of rhythm, and once she heard a song she could repeat it. But even with these natural gifts in her favor the self-taught Kate worked hard, always seeking to give a better performance.

Knowing how important it was for an audience to understand every word, she practiced enunciation, often reciting the words to herself. To get ideas on interpretation she attended concerts, studied recording, listened to artists on the radio, but she was never imitative in her style. Practicing, criticizing, correcting errors in her own work, she insisted that each note be clear, pure and in tune.

With accompanists Kate was a stern taskmaster. "It should go *umpty voom veevo*," she would say reproachfully. And that's the way it had to be even if it took fifteen or twenty rehearsals. Quite capable of bossing the boys in the orchestra on matters of rhythm, volume or tempo, the good-natured, jolly Kate could get tough if things started to slip out of line.

Kate even bossed the Philadelphia Orchestra. At rehearsal things went badly. Kate shook her head gloomily. Then practically pushing the famous conductor, Stokowski, aside, she directed until she got what she wanted. Stokowski, who had felt having Kate sing with the symphony was about on a par with asking the distinguished musicians to play "pop" tunes at a fraternity dance, was startled but delighted. The concert was a huge success. Afterwards Stokowski gave Kate a fatherly pat on the shoulder and said, "God gave you that voice. Don't let anyone change it."

No one did. Kate very carefully studied the meaning of the songs she used—she wanted to give the message honestly. If a work was meant to give joy to her listeners, she had to feel joy. She refused to sing songs that didn't fit her, no matter how popular they might be. Frequently

[194]

this meant substituting simple melodies for hot lick rhythms.

Kate and Ted, who possessed a shrewd combination of showmanship and salesmanship, were constantly on the look-out for new ideas for their programs. *Matinee Hour* was a big star-studded daytime broadcast featuring songs, band numbers, a serial story and human-interest features. Each week the audience was taken to some distant city or glamorous spot—Paris for a style show, or Hawaii with the sound of guitars and waves lapping on the sands at Waikiki. The guest star might be a prizefighter, champion wood chopper, hillbilly musician or a big name like Babe Ruth, cartoonist Otto Soglow or Eleanor Roosevelt.

Later Kate and Ted tried a series in which they journeyed from city to city holding auditions to find new and unknown talent. Successful applicants were brought to New York and given a chance on the network program. These "finds" were paid regular rates for their appearance and provided with as good accompanists as if they were professionals. In addition, contestants got a week-long stay in the city with expenses paid. Because the requests that poured in were simply overwhelming, this project had to be scuttled. But Kate continued giving boosts to performers on their way up. Among those who got a start on her show were the cast of the Aldrich Family and Abbot and Costello.

In 1936 Ted Collins originated *Command Appearance*. Its purpose was to honor heroes in everyday life. The radio audience made the nominations. Awards were given to people like Donald Pirie of Cooper, Iowa, who despite a broken arm plunged into the icy waters of a river to rescue an elderly man trapped under a submerged automobile. When the severely flooded Ohio and Mississippi rivers left thousands homeless and destitute in January of 1937, *Command Appearance* award money was diverted to flood sufferers.

Kate, who two years prior to the flood had received public recognition and life membership in the Red Cross for her efforts in fund raising, now collaborated with this organization in every way possible. In response to her moving appeal for relief funds, letters with donations from children, day laborers, bankers and philanthropists came in by the truckload. Not even Kate, a great believer in human love and kindness, had anticipated such generosity.

The effectiveness of Kate's news-casts during the flood gave Ted another idea. Why not continue with news briefs? Kate had misgivings. She liked the idea of urging people to do things, but radio listeners thought of her as a singer; would they take her news-casting seriously? In preparation for this type of program she had to learn to tone down her naturally booming voice. When she sand-wiched in chatty Americanisms along with the news, Ted got another idea. He encouraged Kate to talk about pets, flowers, clean sports—in short the interests of ordinary people. This was Kate's dish. She had always wanted her programs to uplift and inspire. She pored over newspapers and magazines, studied reference books to get material for her program. On the air, as informally as if chatting with a friend, Kate discussed books, music, hobbies, vaca-tions and babies. She denounced child labor, extolled great women, plugged loyalty to democracy, crusaded for peace, "Talk, think, hope peace," she urged her listeners. People liked the sincerity of Kate the philosopher as much as they had liked Kate the contralto. Kind and sympathetic, she was the sort of person with whom one could have a heart-to-heart talk about a son who had just won a scholarship to college or a husband who drank too much.

People began writing to Kate about their problems. Although preparations for the show left little spare time, she tried at first to answer all mail personally, operating on the philosophy that "The best we can do is to go through life trying to be happy and helping those we meet along the way." On her typewriter Kate pecked out hundreds of encouraging and heartening answers. But the fan mail began to reach staggering proportions. Even with Ted's help, Kate couldn't keep up with it. They hired a secretary who speeded things up by classifying the mail in bins with markings such as Request for Photograph, Autograph, Recipes, Appearances, but finally most of the correspondence had to be passed along to a staff of five secretaries. Letters ranged in subject matter from how to bake a chocolate cake to how to break into radio. Some were begging letters from people who wanted clothing, automobiles or money. A number were sales letters high-pressuring Kate to buy a gold mine, oil well, yacht, an heirloom or an invention. In one instance the salesman offered a lion cub for sale.

Only a small percentage of letters came from cranks or critics who disapproved of Kate's choice of songs or the way she dropped g's on word endings. A far greater number were from people wanting either to get or to give a little friendliness and encouragement.

Kate's favorite letters were those from children. They might be scribbled in pencil and bristle with misspelled words, but they were sincere and were often accompanied by some small donation, a drawing of a pet or of Kate.

Messages like, "Dear Kate: I am only sending twenty-five cents for some poor little hungry child," meant more to her than medals, citations or awards.

But Kate didn't give all her attention to letter writing, or even to news-casting; she kept on singing. Because she was a sure-fire song plugger, her recordings sold by the thousands. When Irving Berlin composed "God Bless America," he gave Kate the exclusive right to use it. She sang it for the first time on Armistice Day, 1938. It became an instant hit. Both Kate and Irving Berlin refused any of the profits, assigning them to Boy and Girl Scouts and other organizations.

Kate has always been generous with her money, talents and time. With her arms loaded with dolls for youngsters or flowers for shut-ins, she became a familiar figure at orphans' homes and hospitals. Countless times she encouraged people who felt beaten to try again. There have been a few instances when moochers have taken advantage of Kate's generosity, but she believes that most people are fundamentally good.

In between radio chats, recording sessions, benefit shows, hospital visits and tours, Kate found time to write a book, *Living in a Great Big Way*. Upon its publication in 1938 Kate said it was the hardest job she had ever done. Autobiographical, it includes not only an account of Kate's career, but much that is entertaining and informative. For those who yearn for a singing career in radio, Kate offers valuable advice. She underlines the necessity for devoting time and energy to preparation. She does not believe that getting to the top is a matter of luck. "Nobody was waiting at the stage door to push little Kathryn Elizabeth Smith into magic success overnight . . . You must work, work, work, if you're to be fit for your chance when it comes." Coupled with that is the necessity for an unswerving belief in that work and the need for striving. You must be able to stand up in the face of disappointments. There must be singleness of purpose and self-discipline. Dissipation, late hours, over-eating of rich foods, a lot of social engagements and outside interests—these are not for the person who wants to be a success. Since the voice reflects the physical condition, a singer cannot afford to smoke, drink or get less than eight hours of sleep a night. Good grooming and posture are important. You must be alert. When you're on the air there is no time for mistakes and corrections. Kate believes young singers should complete their schooling before heading for the big city. Since you're almost sure to experience a period of waiting for an opening, it is unwise to leave the old home town without some reserve fund.

"Don't depend on influence," Kate warns. Influence may get you an audition, but to stay on the air you have to be able to deliver the goods. For that reason, Kate thinks you should be very sure you have outstanding talent before trying big time. You must sing better than countless others. "And you must know what you're feeling and be honest in its expression." She advises young singers to get all the experience possible singing at schools, churches, amateur shows, on local radio stations. These appearances will develop poise and assurance. If your voice is superior you'll get fan mail, and the local manager is almost certain to inform someone on the network. "Big things," says Kate, "are an accumulation of little things. Big successes are only made up of a series of small successes."

Big successes were already coming Kate's way by the time her book was finished. To handle her rapidly increasing income and business affairs the Kated Corporation, combining the names of Kate and Ted, was formed. Its staff not only managed Kate's affairs, but sponsored radio programs, promoted youthful basketball teams, backed charitable projects.

In 1939 Kate was invited to the White House to sing for the King and Queen of England. When George VI heard she was to be there he asked, "Isn't she the girl who sings about the moon and the mountain?"

Through singing and serving, by 1940 Kate was topping all the radio polls in the country. The next year the General Federation of Womens' Clubs named her an outstanding woman pioneer in the field of radio.

During World War II Kate's campaign in behalf of the Red Cross netted four million dollars, for which she was awarded the Legion of Valor medal. In addition to her Red Cross activities she sold millions of dollars' worth of bonds, launched four ships and fourteen bombers and sang at dozens of patriotic rallies. At her own expense she traveled upwards of ninety thousand miles entertaining troops.

As young men who had gone forth to war healthy and self-assured began returning wounded and weary, Kate visited thousands of veterans in hospitals. In gratitude for her songs and sympathy, patients at Edward Hines, Jr. Hospital in Illinois made a belt for her from links of cellophane—each link was autographed by the man who made it. The American Legion gave her honorary membership in the organization.

When television was launched, sponsors wondered if Kate would continue to be a standout. On radio she had sold millions of dollars' worth of cigars, automobiles, tea and cake flour for various sponsors. She had been a spectacular audience-getter. But the muscular, broad-shouldered, two-hundred-and-thirty-pound Kate wasn't exactly the pin-up type.

Rich, famous, successful, Kate could have afforded to take life easy and skip the tests to which television would put her. Instead, she worked harder than ever. Her motive was not making money to add to an already sizeable fortune; Kate doesn't believe success should be reckoned in terms of dollars and cents. To her, money is of little value compared to the deep magic of the woods, the splendor of a sunset or peace of mind. But she found the scope, sweep and bigness of television exhilarating. The new problems it brought—stage-setting, lighting, make-up—challenged her. Just piecing together a show meant hours of intensive planning, but Kate entered into the preparation of scripts and hectic rehearsals with a zestful enthusiasm that brought cooperation from technicians and everyone connected with her show.

When Kate made her television debut viewers saw a woman who was stout but who had a peaches-and-cream complexion and lovely eyes. All the friendliness and personal charm radio listeners had grown accustomed to were plainly visible. Calm and natural, she never missed a cue. Shortly after that, *Kate Smith Speaks* zoomed to top rating.

Kate is appreciative of honors, but dismisses her achievements by saying she makes no claim to being exceptional and that she's had a lot of help from sympathetic, understanding people like Ted Collins. It is the regard of everyday folks that means most to her—not fame.

When she insists, "I'm just a plain, simple woman," she isn't playing a role. In spite of the millions that Kate has made, she lives rather modestly. She did indulge herself in a number of dresses for T.V. shows, but the suggestion that she purchase a mink coat struck her as a sheer extravagance.

In her sunny, frilly New York apartment, Kate likes to retreat to the kitchen, roll up her sleeves and toss together a meal. She has an enviable reputation for concocting delicacies like spoon bread, chocolate cake, lobster stew, chiffon pumpkin pie. Although she enjoys good food, Kate's appetite is not excessive. For years her lunch consisted of two red apples.

Scattered about her apartment are evidences of her collecting hobbies—Dresden figurines, antiques, first editions, early American glassware, perfume bottles. Kate started collecting perfume because she likes beautiful, unusual bottles. Friends sent them in every size, shape, color. Kate also has a collection of autographs and originals of famous cartoons.

Raising flowers is one of her hobbies. As she tends lilies and azaleas on the terrace she shouts greetings at women in nearby penthouses. Kate always has pets. These have ranged from a cocker spaniel to a parrot that greeted visitors with, "Hello, lady."

Her idea of a pleasant evening is to have friends in for bridge or canasta with the radio or t.v. booming full blast. "Hospitality," she says, "is putting warmth and sincerity into 'I'm glad you came.'" Although she enjoys dancing, Kate has never gotten over her dislike for night clubs. She is enthusiastic about football, basketball, baseball. At games fans have often been delighted to hear Kate yelling raucously, "Mow 'em down!"

Usually she summers at her house at Lake Placid. Because she likes to chat with shopkeepers and customers, she does her own shopping. One of her favorite diversions is going out on the lake with her super speedboat which she pilots with reckless abandon, banking and skidding in sharp hairpin turns. A better-than-average swimmer, she also plays a good game of tennis and a slam-bang game of golf. To acquire her skills she practiced tenaciously. As for hiking, Kate usually prefers to cover ground sitting in her limousine, urging the chauffeur to greater speed. In the winter, Kate enjoys bobsledding and skiing through landscape looking like a frosty Christmas card. She has no great urge to conquer the steepest slopes, but considers just being alive in all the white beauty a breath-taking experience. Kate also ice skates like a demon.

Non-sports hobbies include knitting, crocheting and photography. Kate especially likes snapshots that serve as a reminder of some happy occasion, but one of the best shots she ever made was of a disastrous fire. When the cry of Fire! went up in the night while Kate was vacationing in Hot Springs, Arkansas, she grabbed her camera instead of her street clothes and rushed outside. Some of her pictures of the fire were so good they were used in the newspapers the following day, but Kate's clothes went up in flames.

Whether taking pictures, swimming, appearing on television or singing for royalty, Kate is herself. That is one of the secrets of her having been one of the world's most cited women. Another is the way she persisted in singing despite reverses and handicaps. A less courageous person would have given up in the face of excess weight, parental opposition, loneliness, sarcasm and ridicule. It took years of painful experiences to develop the philosophy that, "All handicaps are will-o'-the-wisps we build within our own minds. They go away when we stop thinking about them."

As for the striving connected with her career she says, "There is happiness in living, learning, studying, working and loving—doing the best I can in my own small orbit."

Probably more Americans have listened to Kate Smith via radio and TV than to any other woman. But more than in her singing, Kate's great talent lies in her sensitivity to what needs to be said and done. This accounts for her great power to inspire donations for dolls for the needy, war relief, the Community Chest, firemen's pensions or aid to crippled children. Because she is never afraid of being called sentimental, she speaks from the heart and no appeal ever goes unanswered. Kate has received the keys to scores of cities. In 1947 she was given the Brotherhood Award by the National Conference of Christians and Jews. Time and again she has been listed in national polls as an outstanding woman, and in a 1953 Gallup Poll she was rated as one of the world's ten most admired women.

Gay, high-spirited, she gives off a sense of radiant well-being and contagious joy. There have been plenty of valleys in Kate's life, but she prefers to dwell on the high places. Through her great drive to sing and serve, Kate has become a sort of symbol of some of the best things in American life—sportsmanship, generosity, good-will. No wonder President Roosevelt once introduced her by saying, "This is Kate Smith. This is America."

# 9: MARGUERITE HIGGINS

## Queen of Trench and Typewriter

Marguerite Higgins' determination to be tops in whatever she does had its roots in her childhood. If she took ballet lessons or played the violin, her mother expected her to be a star. A report card that did not show straight A's caused a crisis at home. As a result, Marguerite developed a fierce, competitive drive. Focusing this drive on journalism led her into exciting and dangerous situations, accounts of which won her many awards and the title of America's foremost woman journalist.

Marguerite was born in Hong Kong, China, where her tall, handsome, Irish-American father was Assistant Freight Manager of the Pacific Mail Steamship Company. Marguerite's first words were spoken in Cantonese, a dialect taught her by her Chinese amah. From her French mother, who had met Mr. Higgins in a bomb shelter during World War I, Marguerite picked up a workable French vocabulary. When she was five the Higgins family moved to Oakland, California, and Marguerite promptly forgot her smattering of Chinese; but the classic French, Americanized French and French-accented English she heard at home made it hard for her to master English. Having her mother take her off to France periodically, where she had no chance to practice English, didn't help any.

One day Marguerite saw some neighborhood youngsters

playing gutter-tag, a game frowned upon by Mrs. Higgins, but permitted because the street, a dead-end, was relatively safe. Eagerly she hurried to join the gang. But as she came running up to them the children stopped their game and began intoning, "Marguerite's a Chinaman." Their chanting went on with such phrases as "dirty Chink."

"I'm not a Chinaman," Marguerite shrieked indignantly. "Liar! Liar!"

"Dirty Chinaman!" her tormentors screamed back.

Marguerite retreated homeward. Her parents assured her that she was just as much American as the others, but Marguerite had a hard time convincing her playmates. And because she wanted her parents to be like other parents in the neighborhood, she suffered when her mother spoke French or exhibited quaint mannerisms.

The Higgins home was far from being an island of peace. Mr. Higgins was a moody, high-tempered man. Mrs. Higgins was a very emotional woman who often became disturbed and sometimes collapsed in a faint. Marguerite became so used to crises that she met them in a calm, almost numb sort of way.

To finance her daughter's enrollment in the fashionable Anna Head School, Mrs. Higgins gave French lessons. Later Marguerite got a scholarship. Prodded by fear she might lose it, she studied with such intensity that she had little time left for fun. In moments of rebellion against the grind of scholarship, she sometimes resorted to practical jokes in study hall.

When it came time to think about college, Marguerite narrowed her vocational choices down to two alternatives: she might teach French, or she might become a journalist. One of the things influencing her toward journalism was her curiosity—a curiosity about people and events, but particularly about war. All during her childhood her father had talked about his experiences in World War I, but he hadn't dwelt on death and horror the way many writers did. Instead he seemed impressed by companionship, self-sacrifice and dedication. Marguerite reasoned that as a journalist she might have the chance to see for herself what war was really like.

At the University of California she made an excellent scholastic record, but she was haunted by the fear that after she graduated there wouldn't be any place for her. America was in the grip of a depression. Marguerite had heard about breadlines and knew college graduates who worked at any kind of job they could get—even the most menial tasks. Her own failure to get any kind of summer work at all heightened her worries. After she graduated from the university with high honors, her contributions to a college newspaper, the *Daily Californian,* helped her to get a temporary job on the Vallejo *Times Herald.* But what she really wanted was a job in big-time journalism.

That the odds were against her, Marguerite well knew. It was 1941 and war industries were booming, but newspapers had not yet fully recovered from the crippling effects of the depression. Furthermore, competitive journalism was considered strictly a man's field, and editors were still wary of college-trained reporters. Marguerite was only twenty and had had no experience in rough-and-tumble reporting.

But having set a goal for herself, she never swerved. She stormed one office after another in the West and Midwest with no success. Despite discouragement she decided to try in New York City. She arrived with seven dollars in cash, one suitcase of clothing and a letter of introduction to an aunt and uncle living on Long Island.

That Marguerite chose the New York *Herald Tribune* for her first assault was largely accidental. A stranger in New York, she asked a newsdealer in Times Square, "Where is the nearest metropolitan newspaper?"

He pointed out the *Herald Tribune* building. Clutching a scrapbook in which samples of her work had been pasted, Marguerite, who looked even younger than she was, took the elevator for the editorial office. When she got off the elevator she noticed men she supposed to be reporters brushing past the receptionist's desk. Brashly Marguerite joined their ranks. Panic struck her when she saw the huge brightly-lighted office with rows and rows of desks. Back of each desk was a pair of eyes that she felt sure must be centered on her sky-blue gabardine suit. Shakily she approached the desk of the tall man pointed out to her as City Editor Engelking, who had a reputation for having a colossal temper.

Before the surprised Mr. Engelking had a chance to ask any questions, Marguerite was blurting out details of her past and present. When she handed him the scrapbook the editor looked at the clippings politely. He didn't offer her a job, but he did say that a number of newspapermen were being drafted because of World War II and suggested that she stop back in a month.

It was August. The resourceful Marguerite decided to enter Columbia University for advanced courses in journalism. As a student she could keep her living expenses lower than if she had to live in an apartment and she could finance them with a part-time job. Then when the *Herald Tribune* had an opening she would be available.

Some weeks later Marguerite heard that a fellow student, Murray Morgan, who had been serving as university correspondent for the *Herald Tribune*, had taken another position. Breathlessly she hurried to the *Herald Tribune* office to try to convince Engelking to appoint her as successor. Murray had recommended her, but the editor regarded her in a brooding silence. Finally he asked, "Well, do you think you could start today?"

Marguerite could. Eventually she earned a position on the regular staff. The excitement of actually being with the *Tribune,* carrying her own police and press card, left her starry-eyed. In exuberant letters home she described her apartment and job, which she was sure was the best in the city and much easier than schoolwork.

Her first assignment on the regular *Tribune* staff turned out happily. Since it was the hottest June Sunday in three years she had been told to get a story on the weather. Prowling around trying to think of an angle that would be more interesting than thermometer readings, beach crowds or heat prostrations, Marguerite strolled into the zoo keeper's office in Central Park. He was at the moment telephoning for a fire truck to spray down a South American jaguar, a victim of sunstroke.

Marguerite's exclusive story and a picture of Rosita, the jaguar overcome by heat, appeared in the next issue of the *Herald Tribune.*

But Marguerite soon discovered that getting a who, what, when and why story printed wasn't always that easy. Much of her time was spent in drills on fundamentals. She learned, as she would have on any newspaper, that one has to be accurate—guesswork is not tolerated and a misplaced comma can be fatal. Even though she trained herself to check and double check spellings, names, initials, facts, Marguerite made her share of boners and drew tirades from the boss. Sometimes her purple prose had to be cut or toned down by the rewrite men. But she didn't flaunt hurt feelings and she tried to accept criticism as an opportunity to learn. Only occasionally did Marguerite get exciting stories to cover. As a cub reporter she had to do a lot of leg work chasing up and down alleys or being snubbed by office boys while choice assignments went to the veteran newspapermen. Frequently she was given a handful of obituary notices and told to check to see if the deceased person merited a story. About one in two thousand was a real lead. Many days she had to sit around just waiting for news to break.

On one occasion being passed over proved to be a stroke of luck. The day of the Hartford circus fire, one of the biggest disasters of the decade, the news came in about 3 p.m., when only two reporters were in the office. Marguerite's graphic account of the tragedy in which many lost their lives stirred thousands of readers.

When in search of information, Marguerite was as persistent as a bloodhound, a tendency which was strengthened by the fact that her editor made reporters feel anything was preferable to reporting in without the facts.

Her single-minded zeal for demonstrating she was up to working out problems on her own resulted in several scoops while Marguerite was still a cub reporter. One of these was an interview with James Caesar Petrillo, head of the musician's union. Petrillo was newsworthy because of his efforts to insure musicians a percentage on sales of recordings played over the air and in juke boxes, but the gruff labor czar resisted interviews.

Instead of risking rebuff by telephoning for an appointment with Petrillo, the aggressive Marguerite wheedled his room number from a Waldorf Astoria telephone operator. When she knocked on Petrillo's door, a voice from inside growled, "Who is it?"

"Miss Higgins," answered the flustered Marguerite. Opening the door she found Petrillo in bathrobe and pajamas. It developed that Petrillo had mistaken Marguerite for the maid, but he let her stay for an interview.

As World War II progressed, Marguerite became interested in going overseas as a foreign correspondent. She wanted to be in on the making of history. But editors and journalists in general were of the opinion that the front line was no place for a woman. Marguerite determinedly began harassing every person she thought might get her into Europe. In her favor she had a record of good reporting and a fine educational background. She spoke French fluently, some German and had studied both Russian and Spanish. Friends on the *Tribune* who knew Marguerite's background plugged for her appointment. However, nothing seemed to come of their efforts, and it looked as if the war would be over before Marguerite got overseas.

Finally in August of 1944 word came that she was going abroad as correspondent for the *Tribune's* London and Paris bureaus. She was in London only a short time. In February 1945 she walked into Paris' Hotel Scribe feeling very self-conscious in her freshly pressed olive-drab uniform. The veteran war correspondents, wearing metal insignia and sauntering around the lobby which was strewn with helmets, musette bags and typewriters, all seemed to know each other and their work. They practically ignored Marguerite, making her feel almost as different and set apart as she had the time playmates had jibed her about being Chinese. Their attitude was clear—this was a man's world.

Wistfully appraising their self-assurance, Marguerite suddenly realized that in Paris there would be no city editor to hand out assignments, no copy editor to check mistakes. It would be sink or swim. She hadn't been scared before, but she was now.

Because she was a beginner overseas, Marguerite had to stay in Paris, a limitation which made her impatient. Even so, she didn't intend to follow the example of the veterans who were almost making this a vacation. Marguerite became a cyclone of energy. She read all the French newspapers and the Agence France Presse, the French wire service, but she did not let the matter rest there. If she wanted to send out a story she made direct contact with the ministry or individual involved. At first there was a tendency on the part of some governmental officials to brush her off, but Marguerite's persistence and the excellent quality of her work won them over. Male journalists who had tended to regard women reporters as qualified only to edit society or fashion news, menus or advice to the lovelorn began to take notice.

There were times when Marguerite wished someone had written a book on how to be a foreign correspondent, but schooled as she was in shifting for herself and not stopping at second best, she managed to meet each crisis as it came. She never allowed herself to be deflected from her goal, which was to learn her job and do it well.

Just as the Rhine River was being crossed, the Eighth Air Force announced it planned to fly six correspondents to the front to view bombed areas inside Germany. To Marguerite this looked as if it might be her last chance to get to the front. She immediately marshaled arguments for being included. Later, as a member of a mobile press group traveling by plane and jeep, she visited many sectors and was flown into Frankfurt while much of the city was still in enemy hands. For press headquarters she and her colleagues requisitioned a bomb-blasted house.

When the Seventh Army rolled into the heart of Austria and Germany, Marguerite was with them. She was only about eleven kilometers from the notorious Dachau prison camp when she heard a rumor that liberation of the inmates was close at hand. To be the first reporter at the camp immediately became her goal. The hitch was that the territory between her and Dachau was still held by the Germans. Marguerite talked things over with Sergeant Peter Furst of *Stars and Stripes,* who was a man possessing both courage and get-up-and-go. They decided that few Germans had any fight left in them and that they would risk jeeping to Dachau.

Marguerite was encouraged by the white flags draped in the German villages, but a chill shivered down her spine every time she saw a truckload of soldiers. All along the way German infantrymen insisted on surrendering to the two Americans until the jeep was full of rifles, pistols and grenades.

Arriving at the town of Dachau, which was several miles from the actual camp, Marguerite and Sergeant Furst learned that American and German forces were still fighting, but that someone had reported a white flag was flying at the camp.

Marguerite and the sergeant detoured around the fighting and headed for the camp's main administrative buildings. There the German S.S. general in charge of the camp stood holding aloft a white surrender flag. In a hurry to get to the enclosure where prisoners were kept, Marguerite and the sergeant told the general to surrender to American officers who would be coming along any minute.

A guard was assigned to escort the two Americans. One hazard remained. The watchtower guards weren't in a mood to surrender. Marguerite, who had hopped out of the jeep first when they reached the watchtower area, looked up and saw rifles at ready and a machine gun trained on her. Acting in sheer desperation she called, *"Kommen Sie her, bitte."* (Come here, please.) Fortunately all twenty-two of them came, surrendering their weapons.

Marguerite proceeded to the enclosure, where she encountered pandemonium. The emaciated prisoners crawled, hobbled and ran about in hysterical frenzy. Except for the intervention of a Catholic priest, Marguerite might have been crushed to death by their embraces. Even so she was somewhat battered and bruised. The grimness of the sights at Dachau, the shocking stories of brutality and horror would have overwhelmed Marguerite had it not been that her attention was focused on getting a story that would build a case against the Nazis. Because there was a deadline to be met she concentrated on journalistic details, omitting much of the gruesome and dramatic material at hand. Although she felt the story was inadequate, it ultimately won a prize from the New York Newspaper Womens' Club for the best foreign correspondence of 1945.

Both Marguerite and Sergeant Furst were relieved when the Forty-second and Forty-fifth Divisions arrived, although it meant some temporary discomfort. A brigadier general reached through the iron grillwork of the gate into the enclosure, grabbed Marguerite by the collar and shook her thoroughly, meanwhile demanding, "Don't you know the place is raging with typhus?" The general also berated her and the sergeant for having come in ahead of the army without orders.

Apparently all was forgiven when Marguerite and Sergeant Furst helped quell an uprising a few hours later.

The rioting began when prisoners found that instead of release they faced quarantine until they could be screened for typhus. Over the loudspeaker Marguerite, speaking in German, made explanations, gave reassurances and urged the prisoners to be patient. Later, as a result of the roles Marguerite and Sergeant Furst played that day at Dachau, both received army campaign ribbons for outstanding service under difficult conditions.

Ten days after the Dachau incident, while Marguerite was with the Third Division headquarters at Nazi Joachim von Ribbentrop's beautiful chateau, the German phase of World War II ended. By way of celebration, General O'Daniel gave a party. At midnight, red and blue flames, tracer bullets and anti-aircraft guns shook the castle and stabbed into the darkness.

During a press conference held at von Ribbentrop's chateau, Marguerite met George Reid Millar, an extremely good-looking and also gifted correspondent for the London *Daily Express*. Millar, who held a degree in architecture, had a distinguished and awesome war record. At first Marguerite, who was, with accustomed determination, ferreting out stories as told by top Nazis like Field Marshal Hermann Wilhelm Goering or women members of Hitler's army, didn't pay much attention to Millar. But gradually as she and George tracked down stories together, Marguerite found out that he was very versatile—he could fly a plane, rumba, order skilfully from a French menu. His life had been packed with unusual experiences and he was an exciting contrast to people who did things in a routine way. For the first time Marguerite had a love interest that competed with her desire to get her by-line on the front page.

But there were many subjects on which Marguerite and

George disagreed. He took great delight in criticizing Americans and their manners or actions. Marguerite's reactions were peppery, especially when he made the accusations in terms of "you Americans." They argued over attitudes toward the Germans. Their opinion of journalism differed—George maintained it was often a tawdry and inconsequential business. They couldn't agree on where they would live after their marriage.

One day while they were in Paris, George went off to London for an indefinite stay. Marguerite missed him terribly. Some days later he wired that he wasn't coming back. For Marguerite there was only one remedy—work. She turned to it with such intensity and determination that there was no time for brooding or boredom.

During the next few weeks she prowled through Czechoslovakia. It was a miserable personal experience to see a nation whose pride had once been in its intricate cathedrals and fragile glassware, become a supplier of Russian needs and lose its freedom. As days passed, Marguerite saw the people become paralyzed with fear and nerve-wracking uncertainty as to their fate. She herself had the experience of being awakened at 5 A.M. by security police who broke into her hotel room demanding her passport and thumbing through her notebooks.

When Marguerite announced her intention of driving into Poland, her colleagues objected. "There's still civil war in some areas," one of them said grimly.

The drive to Warsaw was tame, but the city itself, with acres of rubble and sooty, shattered buildings, was a depressing sight. At the Hotel Polonia, where she arrived cold and tired, Marguerite had to argue three hours before she got a room which had a peculiar orange-brown lighting effect. Rats, the fattest of which she named Hermann

Goering, scurried about the room and supervised her typing of news dispatches.

As she went about interviewing factory workers, intellectuals, priests, Marguerite saw the terrors of the Nazi police state being replaced by the terrors of the Russian police state—threats, beatings, imprisonment, death.

In the late summer of 1947 Marguerite was named chief of the New York *Herald Tribune's* Berlin Bureau. She was then twenty-six, had been overseas three years and had turned out more front page stories than any other correspondent.

The appointment, though not unhoped for, was unexpected. Marguerite had thought a man would get the assignment. Because much of the city lay in ruins and there were acute shortages of food and fuel, Berlin was considered a hardship post. But Marguerite figured Berlin would be a hot spot in the news, and since news was her business she was excited about the promotion. Being chief meant more money, more prestige, a secretary, a cook and her own house to live in that boasted a library and eventually her own collection of records.

But Marguerite was so busy garnering facts and writing the Berlin story that she had little time to enjoy her new luxuries. To her usual determination was added the fear that if she made a mistake her coveted job might be taken away.

She had barely gotten herself organized when the Soviets blockaded Berlin in their attempt to force the Western Allies out of the city. Some believed the Americans, including the press corps, should quit, but General Clay, head of the American Army of Occupation, decided his countrymen should stay even if it meant war.

Getting out news on the blockade seemed a never-ending task. Because Soviet releases kept coming through until midnight, many of Marguerite's stories had to be written in the pre-dawn hours and were often typed by candlelight, since power failures were frequent. She had two secretaries now, one for daytime, one for night. Into them Marguerite instilled some of her own reportorial zeal. They soon learned that any failure on their part would arouse Marguerite's ire. A major scoop by a competitor was a personal disaster.

Despite hardships Marguerite loved the Berlin assignment. The blockade was a fascinating test of international strength; and in writing stories about this war of nerves, stories that would be read by the man on the street, Marguerite felt as if she had some small share in the making of history. The courageous stand of General Clay, who refused to be bullied, the efficiency of American planes bringing food and coal to supply the city despite the blockade, increased Marguerite's pride in being an American.

Facing threats of starvation or of war, the Americans in Berlin were staunch, cheerful and unusually considerate of each other. They flocked to the Press Club to play tennis, chat and share their joys and sorrows.

Although Marguerite had little time for recreation, she occasionally invited friends in for dinner or to listen to her records—the best collection in Berlin. The phonograph often gave out weird sound effects, since it ran on electricity manufactured by a small undependable generator her secretary Ellen had scrounged, but it didn't spoil Marguerite's pleasure in the music of *South Pacific* or the Beethoven *Violin Concerto.*

On occasion Marguerite had to desert her guests because of some unexpected crisis in the news. There were some who felt her devotion to her work was a little fantastic, but she stuck stubbornly to her news writing, determined that nothing should interfere.

A riot at which Marguerite was an innocent bystander did interfere temporarily, however. Returning from a fact-gathering foray on an anti-Russian demonstration at a gate between the Russian and British sector of Berlin, Marguerite got caught in a mob. Accidentally she was pushed into a pile of rubble filled with jagged bricks and bits of glass. Laceration added to a rash which had been plaguing her for some time resulted in a serious skin disorder. A doctor ordered her to a hospital in Switzerland.

For a few days Marguerite almost enjoyed her enforced rest. But then she received a disturbing telephone call from a colleague in Berlin who told her there was talk of her being transferred to Paris on the basis that she was overtired, too competitive, overeager and too intense. Marguerite was furious. She decided to act as if nothing had happened and to reclaim her job immediately from Steve White, who had been sent to substitute for her. Marguerite's appearance in Berlin occasioned some surprise, but she got to stay on awhile longer.

In 1950, having recently returned from leave to America, Marguerite expected a two-year stint in Berlin, but she got word she was to be transferred to the Tokyo Bureau. The New York *Herald Tribune* had good reasons for making the change. Marguerite had been on the same job since the summer of 1947, and freshness of viewpoint is important to a journalist. Besides, Joe Newman, who had been in Moscow, wanted the Berlin post and his standing was high in the New York office.

Things had been very dull on the Far Eastern front and

Marguerite was reluctant to leave Germany. But when she protested, the foreign editor told her she'd have to go, whether she liked it or not.

In Tokyo, where she lived in a small humid room at the Press Club, Marguerite longed for her Berlin house, her cook, for secretary Ellen, her phonograph. But most of all she missed the exhilaration of doing big stories.

After her first week in Japan, Marguerite heard that on May thirtieth there would be a national election in Korea, only a four-hour flight away. She arrived in Kaesong several days ahead of the elections and got a good story, but she saw a bigger one shaping up—the Chinese Reds based in North Korea were already firing mortars into Kaesong.

Twenty-five days after she filed her first Eastern dispatch, war broke in Korea. Excited by the prospect of a big journalistic opportunity, Marguerite was determined to get there, and although military authorities opposed her appointment she finally won her personal crusade.

Two days after she arrived in Korea the Reds launched a brutal invasion of the southern half of the country. The retreating South Koreans became confused and blew up the bridge over which the jeep in which Marguerite was riding was supposed to escape. While the military personnel frantically sought an alternative, Marguerite sat down on the ground to compose a news story.

The stranded party later crossed the river on a raft, hiked a rugged mountain trail and were finally picked up by a jeep. At intervals, Marguerite pecked out the details on her typewriter, including a graphic description of the refugees—hungry children, pitiful oldsters with huge bundles on their heads and women with babies bound papoose-style on their backs.

After a few days at the front, Marguerite—dubbed

"Maggie" by the G.I.'s—was ordered by one of the military authorities to leave Korea on the basis that a woman didn't belong where standards of dress, language and sanitation were so primitive.

Maggie was flown to Tokyo. There she hurried directly to General MacArthur, with whom she had once wangled an interview. Remembering the competent way in which Maggie had handled the material he had given her, the general was both friendly and sympathetic. He assured her that she could return. As an added bonus he gave Maggie a private word of encouragement and wired her boss saying her journalistic capacities were held in high esteem.

Back in Korea again, Maggie adopted G.I. dress—regulation shirt, trousers, fatigue cap and tennis shoes. Knowing that being a woman made her a target for comment, she leaned over backward in not asking favors or privileges. She refused a cot and slept on the ground or on a table at press headquarters. To cut down on luggage she carried only a toothbrush, towel, lipstick, comb and typewriter. She learned to scrounge for necessary supplies, to douse herself with flea powder and hit a foxhole in approved G.I. style. "I'm not in Korea as a woman, but as a war correspondent," she told those who offered to pamper her. Although she described herself as a "lousy shot," she did consent to carry a gun.

Feeling it was her duty to get as vivid and first-hand coverages as possible, the pert and fearless Maggie jeeped, often in the company of Keyes Beech, Chicago *Daily News* correspondent, to hot spots where some of her colleagues were reluctant to go. Some who were antagonistic to the idea of a woman at the front charged that Maggie was foolhardy. Actually it was her practice to brief herself carefully on the terrain, the chances of survival, and then figure out coverage accordingly. The times when it looked as if she might get herself killed were the results of unexpected developments. One of these unplanned incidents came when the Communists infiltrated the lines at night and staged a surprise attack. A machine gun spurted only a few yards away from where Maggie was eating breakfast.

When an amphibious assault was made behind North Korean enemy lines at Inchon Harbor, Marguerite went along in a steel-sided landing craft, instead of sticking to the relative safety of a destroyer. With bullets sputtering and whining around her, she hit the sea wall with the fifth wave of invaders and snaked up "Red Beach" on her stomach.

Her reporting of what she experienced at Inchon and elsewhere was hard-hitting and frank—sometimes too frank to please military officials. The Army would have liked to suppress her stories on blunders made by green troops and expensive equipment left behind by panicky Americans in retreat, but Maggie thought the truth should be told even if it bruised.

With professional capability she went right on turning out dispatches that were sometimes exciting, but more often heart-rending in their portrayal of the dismal wastefulness of war. Sometimes Maggie wrote under fire, at other times in the pandemonium of press headquarters where typewriters clattered and reporters yelled their stories into telephones. Nothing, not even bone-aching weariness or injury, diminished her determination to give her best.

Male correspondents resented her scoops. But her undaunted spirit and extraordinary durability in the face of monsoon downpours, jeep upsets or enemy attacks won her the respect of G.I. and general alike, who honored her as "queen of the trench as well as of the typewriter." "Maggie wears mud the way other women wear make-up," said one of her colleagues when someone commented that she was pretty even in combat clothes.

Praised for her courage Maggie explained it by saying, "Curiosity and excitement have outbalanced fear."

Toward the wounded, Maggie showed a selfless devotion. On hot, stuffy trains, on battlefields under fire, she helped to administer plasma. Always she stood in awe of men who, tried beyond endurance, went on enduring.

One of the highlights in the Korean War as far as Maggie was concerned was her participation in the liberation of Seoul in September of 1950. Still dirty and frayed from the fight, Maggie watched while General MacArthur, flanked by top brass, received the keys of the city from the Korean president Syngman Rhee.

Conscious of her bedraggled appearance, Maggie tried to remain inconspicuous, but when MacArthur passed close to her she couldn't resist calling out, "Hi General; congratulations on this victory."

The usually dignified general replied, "Hello, there, tall, dark, and ugly. Come up and see me some time!"

About a month later Maggie got a summons from her office to return home to address the New York *Herald Tribune's* annual forum. After the address Marguerite was besieged by invitations to write books, columns, magazine articles, to appear on TV and to make speeches. In her first thirty days back she had over two thousand requests for public appearances. Although she had come through the Korean War unscathed, the cumulative effects of fatigue, harassing pressures from the public and disappointments in her personal affairs made her ill. And because she was sick she was soon broke.

Bright spots in an otherwise dark period of her life were

various prizes and awards. Women editors of Associated Press member newspapers voted her Woman of the Year. She shared the coveted Pulitzer Prize for "distinguished foreign correspondence" with Homer Bigart, received the Overseas Press Club George Polk Memorial Award for "courage, integrity and enterprise above and beyond the call of duty," and became the first woman to receive the annual "Poor Richard Citation" of the Poor Richard Club of Philadelphia. There were other awards adding up to well over fifty.

During a period of relative inactivity, Marguerite wrote *War in Korea,* which is an account of her experience, but also includes much of her philosophy about war in general. After finishing the book she made a twenty-four city lecture tour.

In 1952 Marguerite married Major General William E. Hall, commander of the Fourth Air Force. Sorrow came to the couple with the death of their baby Sharon when the child was only five days old.

Finding it necessary to supplement her husband's income, Marguerite rejoined the staff of the New York *Herald Tribune.* Her first assignment was to write a syndicated column covering potential tinderboxes in the cold war. Marguerite was still in love with newspaper work, and the prospect of a world-wide tour of inspection excited her, but she regretted the necessity of being away from home and husband for ten weeks.

In Spain at luxurious quarters guarded by gaudily uniformed soldiers, Marguerite interviewed General Franco, who greeted her cordially and worked hard to convince her that Spain was not a police state.

The next lap of her tour took her to Paris, where she interviewed General Eisenhower who was then Supreme

Commander for the North Atlantic Treaty Organization countries. Eisenhower was not so affable as Marguerite had expected. There was no joshing, no breaking of the ice with an anecdote. At times the general was stern, tense, almost scholarly. But Marguerite was impressed by his energy, convictions and faith, and greatly pleased when he gave her his personal copy of *The True Believer*—a book discussing the forces that motivate people to support communism and other -isms.

In East Berlin Maggie talked to youths who were only outwardly Communistic. A fifteen-year-old summed up their attitude by saying, "If we don't join the Communist youth fronts we can't get an education."

In Yugoslavia Marguerite met the square-jawed General Tito, trailed by his German police dog, Tiger. For an interview with the King of Siam she went to Lausanne, Switzerland. Marguerite found little resemblance to the monarch portrayed in the Broadway hit *The King and I*. At the moment the king's biggest concern was how his country could protect itself from Communist China.

In Iran Marguerite had the privilege of attending parliament. Karachi, India, shocked her with its howling children begging for a living and the thousands of people sleeping in the streets. But she was greatly impressed when she met the handsome, graying Nehru, who seemed to have selfless sincerity. A champion of equality for women, he told her how he had to battle traditions in India.

Marguerite arrived in Indo-China in time to visit the French forces before they were captured by communists. The rough and rutty roads reminded her of Korea.

At the modest brick home of Generalissimo Chiang Kai-shek on Formosa, Marguerite was greeted graciously by his wife, looking very smart in a Chinese-style blue silk dress.

While they ate corn on the cob, ordered in honor of Marguerite, the small, slight, dignified Chiang asked many questions about her trip.

Back in Korea once more, Marguerite visited the site of the truce talks at the mud hut village of Panmunjon, where Chinese in quilted jackets and Koreans in Russian-style uniforms sat across the table from the Americans. Although the truce talks were in progress, battles were still being fought and the roads were jammed with refugees and children begging for hand-outs.

How had she managed to interview so many important persons, journalists kept asking after Marguerite's return to America. Intervention of American diplomats and kudos resulting from some of her Korean stories accounted for the opening of some doors, but much of the explanation of her success lay in Marguerite's skill as an interviewer. Before she talked to a celebrity she delved into reference books and periodicals to learn as much as she possibly could about the person and his country so she would have some background and wouldn't have to ask unnecessary questions. Her integrity made those she interviewed know that she could be trusted in matters of craftsmanship and exactness in quotations or expression of viewpoints.

In 1955 Marguerite's second book, *News is a Singular Thing,* was published. It includes a brief account of her childhood and details of her career and crises in personal life. Across the pages march descriptions of colorful people she met, interviewed or worked with.

In each of her books Marguerite has something to say about journalism as a career. She points out that, although it is gratifying, diverting and exciting, it is also exacting. The road to success in this field involves a number of intangibles, but some of the basic requirements she feels are integrity, persistence and strong nerves in the face of crises. Another important requirement is the ability to get to the main source of the news, which usually involves a combination of leg and head work.

For first-rate war coverage, Marguerite would add two more qualifications: capacity for physical endurance and the willingness to take personal risks.

In journalism every sentence, every column is a new test of skill. There can never be any resting on past attainments. "It is a solitary path," says Marguerite. "One must grope alone."

She has a great deal to say about the disadvantages under which women in journalism have to operate. In *War in Korea* she writes, "A women is a target for all kinds of vicious stories—some will claim you get stories because of a nice smile; some men correspondents resent women."

But women have a few advantages too, Marguerite admits. A female journalist, especially one who is assigned to foreign correspondence, is regarded as unique. Good work or a display of courage from a woman wins more acclaim, more publicity than a male correspondent gets.

Whatever the hardships and disadvantages Marguerite would not have traded jobs with anyone. Her enthusiasm ran high when an assignment from the New York *Herald Tribune* for a journalistic foray into Russia coincided with a grant from the Guggenheim Foundation. She had already done considerable research on the subject of negotiating with the Russians.

In the u.s.s.r Marguerite spent a good deal of time riding buses, sitting in parks, visiting in restaurants in the hope of striking up conversations with ordinary Russians. But even then their statements were very cautious and guarded.

Everything seemed to take a long time in Russia, including making a telephone call. In Leningrad she saw shiny new red and white buses and modern buildings, but on the same streets were kerchiefed women in faded, patched cottons sweeping streets with primitive brooms made of twigs. Russian women were also digging ditches and wielding picks and shovels as railroad maintenance workers.

At a style show in Moscow, Marguerite found the dresses peculiar in color and shoddy in quality, but the spectators, many of whom wore boots, cotton stockings, coarse wool clothes, sighed enviously when the models came on the stage.

Food was expensive. For one hard-boiled egg and tea Marguerite paid a dollar. And she was arrested a total of sixteen times for attempts to take photographs. One arrest was the result of her photographing a tomato vendor in a Stalingrad market where a man in a rumpled gray suit unaccountably began yelling, "Spy, spy." Fortunately no detention ever lasted more than five hours, but Marguerite's edginess and uneasiness became more acute than during her days in Korea. Among Russians she interviewed were ballet dancer Ulanova and Olympic champion Galina Zybina.

Upon her return to America Marguerite's observations on her trek through Siberia, Soviet Central Asia, the Caucasus, White Russia and the Ukraine were recorded in a book titled *Red Plush and Black Bread*. Astute and perceptive, Marguerite's writing shows many of the qualities that made her a top-notch correspondent.

When queried as to the Why of her success, Marguerite is likely to respond, "Trouble is news and the gathering of news has been my job."

Actually the Why of her success isn't that simple. To begin with, she had an exuberant vitality, a keen intellect

[228]

and a sleepless curiosity. To these she added a broad education larded with English and history, the capacity for hard work and dogged determination to excel. In her days as a cub reporter she learned how to use her legs and imagination to meet challenges.

Marguerite Higgins has always given journalism the best she had, and that best was very good; but it became even better after she learned that fame and money "have nothing to do, in a positive sense, with happiness." She has found that her greatest happiness came when "working for causes which symbolized purposes beyond the range of personal self-interest." It was through sharing the burdens of war and oppression that Marguerite learned compassion.

After fourteen years of travel Marguerite settled down in Washington, D. C., with her husband Major General William E. Hall. In her home, decorated with treasures collected from all over the world, she enjoys her pets—a dog and a parakeet. Her assignment as White House correspondent for the *Herald Tribune* has been considerably less hectic than foreign posts, but even then Marguerite has stirred up excitement. When the question arose as to whether her endorsement of a certain toothpaste conflicted with the policy of members of the press gallery not to engage in paid publicity or promotion work, Marguerite relinquished her membership.

Whether Marguerite ever accepts another overseas assignment or not remains to be seen. But the fact is that because she writes from the heart she has won a place of unique distinction among women journalists.

# 10: JULIETTE GORDON LOW

## A Friend to All

Juliette Gordon was the kind of child who started things —games, plays, clubs. But the activity which made her famous, the founding of the Girl Scouts, was not begun until she was past fifty-two. Unlike most persons who have made an outstanding contribution, Mrs. Low, up to the time she launched scouting, had lived a glamorous, exciting kind of life usually reserved for story-book heroines.

Juliette was born on Hallowe'en of 1860 in Savannah, Georgia. Her father, a grandson of early settlers in Georgia, served as an officer in the Confederate Army during the Civil War. Mrs. Gordon was a Northerner. One of the first white children born in Chicago, she had grown up at Fort Winnebago where her father, John Harris Kinzie, was a federal government agent for the Winnebago Indians.

Because Juliette was a child with flowerlike charm, her family nicknamed her Daisy. On the grounds of the stately Gordon mansion, gay with camellias, azaleas and flaming pomegranate trees, Daisy and her sister Nellie romped and played all kinds of games. They even made a game of helping their tiny, light-hearted mother care for their baby sister, Alice.

Only two things marred Daisy's happiness. She was often lonely for her father who was away from home because he had to fight in the war. And she disliked being called a Yankee just because her mother had been born a Northerner. Once when a playmate taunted her, quick-tempered Daisy protested hotly, "I'm the rebellest rebel in the whole South."

Daisy was only four the day news came that the Union Army led by General Sherman was just outside Savannah. Hour by hour the sound of the guns came closer. Before long the streets were filled with women and children in flight—some in carriages, some on foot, pushing a few of their choicest belongings on carts or wheelbarrows. Daisy's mother and the family servants worked frantically, hiding or burying the crystal and silver.

A few days later, so early in the morning that Daisy was still half-asleep, she saw endless columns of men in blue uniforms marching past the house. Shortly after that a grim-faced messenger came to the house. "Women and children have been ordered to leave the city," he told Mrs. Gordon.

As she watched her mother sitting primly erect in a dress with lace and furbelows, Daisy saw all the sparkle go from her eyes.

"You may expect a call from your old friend, General Sherman," the messenger said as he was leaving.

While waiting for the general, Daisy and Nellie moved about restlessly in their stiffly starched dresses. They hoped none of their playmates would see a Yankee general come to their house. Daisy half expected a beast with horns, but the general won her over with a gift of sugar which, because of the war, she had never tasted. General Sherman also gave Mrs. Gordon permission to go through enemy lines to see the children's father.

When she returned, Mrs. Gordon told them, "Your father wants me to take you children to your Grandfather and Grandmother Kinzie in Chicago."

The idea of a trip was exciting, but Daisy didn't want to leave her father fighting Yankees, and she wondered what would happen to their house and all her playthings while they were away.

On the boat trip to New York, storms kept the active children from getting out on deck very much. In New York the Gordons took a train west. Some of the railroads in the 1860's were still locally owned, and passengers had to put up with almost as many inconveniences as stage-coach travelers. The Gordons had to change at every ter-minal point, which sometimes meant a long wait in a cold, bare station. Grimy with cinders and exhausted by the long journey, Daisy was glad to get to the home of her grandparents on the outskirts of Chicago. There was an enticing odor of cookies baking as soon as they opened the door.

In the days that followed, Grandmother Kinzie, a round-faced little woman with twinkly eyes, prepared food Daisy had never tasted, or had forgotten because of war short-ages—baked ham, delicious loaves of crusty bread, apple dumplings. At first Daisy saved tidbits she really wanted for herself, planning to send them to her father. When told it would be impossible to get anything to him, she was deeply disappointed.

Daisy loved her grandfather's animals—the dog, cat, cows, horses and a parrot that followed around scolding for crackers and attention. After a cow lost her calf, Daisy put her arms around the animal's neck and wept bitterly. "The cow cried too," she insisted.

Grandfather Kinzie's activities as government agent and paymaster fascinated Daisy almost as much as the animals.

Indians came to Grandfather Kinzie, whom they called Silver Man, not only for pay, but for advice. Sometimes they camped in the yard, which covered a whole square block. Daisy and Nellie never tired of watching powwows, games of LaCrosse and footraces which their tall, slim grandfather often won. Occasionally the Indians brought their womenfolk. Then Daisy, who was a very friendly child, and Nellie would take their dolls and play with the Indian children.

Winter brought new delights. Daisy had never seen snow, and she found playing with sleds and building snowmen and make-believe igloos very exciting. Evenings the children sprawled in front of the fireplace and listened to the wonderful stories Grandfather Kinzie had to tell. Daisy's favorite was about her own great-grandmother, who in childhood had been kidnapped by the Indians and had lived with the tribe for four years. They had named her Little Ship Under Sail.

" 'Little Ship Under Sail,' would be a good name for you," her grandfather told Daisy.

But even with the story-telling and the outdoor fun, the winter seemed long, and Daisy was glad when the cherry trees blossomed and she found hepaticas in the woods. Then one day news came that the war was over. Daisy couldn't believe that the South had lost. Because of her persistent remarks about "mean old Yankees," Grandfather Kinzie became stern. He pointed out how kind Yankees had been to her while she had been living in the North, and tried to get her to see there had been wrongs on both sides.

In late summer Daisy's father, a handsome man with a straight, fine figure, came to Chicago. That night the children sat up long after the lamps had been lighted, listening to what Mr. Gordon had to say. The house was still there, he told them, but his cotton business had been ruined.

Daisy wanted to go home, and yet she hated leaving the Indians, her grandparents and her pets. But armed with some of Grandmother's cookies and scraps of cloth for doll clothes, the sisters started for Savannah with their parents. Back in Georgia, the Gordons found fields seared and meadows without cattle. At their own home all the pots, pans and dishes were gone. Food was scarce. Compared with the way the Gordons had lived before, they were now poor. But Daisy knew there were many who were poorer than they were. Some time after their return, she began hearing about shortages of clothing. "Let's start a club to help," she suggested to some of her playmates. "We'll call it the Helping Hands."

At their first meeting Daisy tried valiantly to teach her friends how to sew, although she had never learned how herself. When a jacket practically fell to pieces on the first fitting, one of the onlookers jeered, "You'd better call yourselves the Helpless Hands."

Gradually things got better for the South and for Daisy's family. As Mr. Gordon rebuilt his business, faded rugs were replaced and new furniture appeared. The family was very happy when a red-haired baby boy named William was born. Later there were two more children, Mabel and Arthur.

Grandmother Gordon, who had come to live with the family, was sometimes a trial to Daisy. Proper pastimes for girls, according to Grandmother, were paper dolls and teas where one was expected to sip cambric tea from a delicate china cup. Daisy much preferred swimming, tennis, or horseback riding. Tender-hearted, she could never bear the thought of an animal in pain or distress. To the Gordon stable she was always bringing half-drowned kittens, hungry dogs, lame crows. On a cold night she got blankets from the guest room, took them to the stable and pinned them around the cow.

Summers in Savannah were hot, and the Gordon children usually spent part of their vacation at their Aunt Elizabeth's (Mrs. W. H. Stiles) home at Etowah Cliffs in northern Georgia. Here, running in and out of the rambling house with a long piazza, there were often as many as twenty cousins.

After a few morning chores, the children spent the rest of the day climbing the sheer cliffs of the Etowah River, swimming or riding horses. When they tired of active games, they sat under the trees in the peach orchard telling stories. Daisy often prodded the others into writing and producing plays. For costumes they had finery stored in a trunk called the circus trunk. Another project was their own magazine, to which Daisy contributed drawings, stories and verse.

When Daisy was fourteen, the family finances having been replenished, she and Nell enrolled in the Stuart Hall Boarding School in Virginia. Daisy had begged to go, but once there she was terribly homesick. However, a stubborn persistence about finishing what she had begun kept her from giving up and going home.

Daisy had genuine artistic talent and found sketching more exciting than parsing sentences or proving theorems. One day in Greek class when she sketched the teacher wearing oversized shoes on the wrong feet, she was severely reprimanded.

Later, when Nell went on to finishing school, Daisy transferred to Edge Hill, conducted by the Misses Randolph, granddaughters of Thomas Jefferson. Here she sketched birds and chipmunks in the woods, worked in oils and ended the year with a medal in painting.

The fall she was seventeen Daisy went to a finishing school in New York run by two Frenchwomen—the Mlles. Mathilde and Fannie Charbonnier. "The Charbs are terribly strict," Daisy wrote to a friend. "All conversation is in French. As for boys—they aren't even allowed near the school."

Week-ends were more exciting. Daisy looked forward to dancing class, where the girls learned such niceties as how to enter a room. Sometimes "the Charbs" took the girls to a concert, an opera or the theater. Occasionally Daisy visited cousins at Newark or Trenton, enjoying teas, dances, sleigh rides. On one occasion she went into a New York hotel, ordered a meal; then, realizing she had forgotten her purse, she fled before the waiter had served her. When she told the story at home, her father, who was very ethical, made her write to the hotel, get the bill and pay it.

Daisy's second year at "the Charbs" was saddened by the death of her sister Alice, whom she had begged to accompany her. After graduation from the school, Daisy spent a short time in New York studying china painting and then returned to Savannah.

The following winter brought a succession of parties, dances, boat races, amateur theatricals. Witty, brilliant, a good dancer, Daisy was in constant demand. The only shadow on her life was a deafness in one ear caused by a mistaken application of nitrate of silver which virtually destroyed one eardrum.

At a ball, Daisy met a young Englishman named William Low. Son of a Savannah-born woman, he had been sent back to America to look after family cotton business interests. Daisy thought he was the most interesting, most handsome man in the world.

Some months later, on December 21, 1886, Daisy and William were married in a church overflowing with guests. Bridesmaids wore the very latest in poke bonnets and basques.

Honeymoon happiness on Saint Catherine's Island was marred by an infection which developed in Daisy's good ear as a result of lodgment of a grain of rice thrown at the time of the wedding. In the process of removing it her hearing was further impaired. Daisy joked about her affliction but felt keenly the loneliness imposed by such a handicap. In the Savannah mansion where Thackeray had written *The Virginians* while visiting America, Daisy took up her housekeeping duties.

The summer following their wedding, the Lows went to England, when they bought a country estate called Wellesbourne, situated in central England among green valleys and winding rivers. Here gay crowds, including English nobility, gathered for house parties, pigeon shoots and southern-style dinners prepared by a cook imported from Georgia.

Daisy, called Juliette by the English, enchanted socialites with her high-spirited energy. She soon had many British friends, despite the fact that her unconventional acts—such as prevailing upon Rudyard Kipling to go salmon fishing in evening clothes, or helping the blacksmith redesign the gates for the estate—sometimes pained her neighbors. She and her husband had a box at the opera, attended plays, banquets, teas, and often visited a hunting lodge they had bought in Scotland where they rode to hounds. Wearing a white satin dress with little festoons of ostrich feathers stitched on the skirt and a six-yard-long train, Juliette was presented at the court of Queen Victoria.

Off and on the Lows visited their house in Savannah, where guests were entertained with tarpon fishing, southern cookery and Negro spirituals. Daisy and William traveled in Europe, Africa, the Orient, frequently being entertained by kings, princes or noblemen. On these trips, William often teased Daisy because of the great mounds of luggage she insisted upon taking. Out of it she would fish up anything from a hot water bottle to a parrot.

Her luxurious life notwithstanding, Daisy's sympathies were always with the underprivileged or unfortunate. Deep-hearted and compassionate, she thought of ingenious ways to help shut-ins or down-and-outers.

As soon as the Spanish-American War broke out, Daisy returned to Savannah. Her father, General Gordon, was serving with the army in Florida. After he had described the shocking lack of care of the wounded, Mrs. Gordon went to Florida to help establish a convalescent hospital near Miami. Daisy volunteered her services also. The weather was hot, the work exhausting, but she never complained. Her wit and charm kept the men in good humor. When food ran short, Daisy, with characteristic energy, got a horse and buggy and scrounged for supplies.

At the end of the war she returned to England, where she found her husband sick. Growing steadily worse, he died in 1905. Daisy tried to go on doing the things she and William had done together, but her social life seemed meaningless. One of her greatest joys at Wellesbourne had been having all the pets she wanted. But now some restlessness kept her from finding satisfaction in them or in her excellence in horsemanship. Hoping art would ease her grief, she spent more and more hours in creative work, while a yapping pekingese kept her company. The products—paintings, sketches, sculptured pieces—were shared with delighted friends. True happiness, Daisy knew, lay in self-forgetfulness, but she seemed unable to achieve it.

Because she loved seeing new places and meeting new people, she began to travel almost incessantly. Frequently she took a niece or nephew with her. But no matter what part of the globe she visited, she always looked forward to Christmas in Savannah, and returned in time for the holidays loaded with carved necklaces, ivory figurines, exotic trinkets for the entire family. The youngsters adored Aunt Daisy, who provided them with pets, invented incredible games and told colorful, fascinating stories of Tibetan priests, Chinese bandits and Japanese geisha girls.

But traveling didn't cure Daisy's restlessness. She felt a growing necessity to give herself to some worthwhile cause. Friends tried to reassure her, pointing out that she wasn't as healthy as she had once been, and that since she had the means for comfortable living she'd better take advantage of it.

When Daisy met Sir Robert Baden-Powell, founder of the Boy Scouts, at a luncheon in 1911, she was fascinated by his activities. "You have made a success of everything, Sir Robert," she exclaimed. "My life has been wasted."

"There are little stars that guide us on," Sir Robert said, "although we do not realize it."

As he went on to tell her how Boy Scouting promoted friendship, built character, gave training in citizenship and various skills, Daisy's imagination was fired. All the time he was talking she kept thinking—girls ought to be in on this too. Finally she asked, "Why should all this be just for boys? Why couldn't there be a similar organization for girls?"

"There is," he replied. Then he described how in 1909 at a Boy Scout rally at the Crystal Palace in London, sisters of the boys had come marching and demanded troops of their own. To meet their need an English Girl Guide program had been launched.

Daisy found out all she could above the movement. A year later she organized a troop of Girl Guides at Glenlyon in Scotland. Most of the girls were from poor homes; several of them walked miles to attend meetings. Daisy decided to teach them practical skills—how to garden; how to cook good, nourishing food; how to spin, weave, raise poultry—things that would help with supporting families. Daisy also gave the girls plenty of chances for parties and fun. Seeing how much Girl Guiding was doing for these girls raised a question in her mind. Why shouldn't American girls enjoy it, too? But first she must get more pointers. Meanwhile, she launched another troop in London.

Finally Daisy felt she'd learned enough from troop leaders and her own experience to start the Girl Guides program in America. Inspired and determined, she sailed for Savannah January 6, 1912, sending a cable ahead, "I'm bringing home the biggest thing yet."

Before Daisy had unpacked, she telephoned her friend, Nina Pape, who headed a girls' school. "Nina, come right over," she urged. "I've got something for the girls of Savannah, and all America and all the world."

But Daisy's friends and family were lukewarm about her plans. Wouldn't the work of setting up the organization be too rugged? "You're fifty-two," they reminded her.

Though they didn't add, and you're partially deaf, Daisy knew they were thinking it.

"And you've had no training in organization, business or finance," a nephew told her. Daisy had to admit that even in handling personal finance since William's death she had been absent-minded and sometimes downright incompetent. Anyone involved in large-scale public work certainly ought to be efficient in handling money. She wouldn't know the first thing about budgeting or fund raising.

Daisy argued with her family and she argued with herself. Except for the work she had done during the Spanish-American War she had to acknowledge that hers had been a pampered life. She hadn't been trained in leadership. But she had the Girl Guiding experience to fall back on. And she had both outdoor and artistic skills she could teach the girls. All the time the arguments were flying back and forth, Daisy kept thinking of a conversation with Sir Robert Baden-Powell in which he had told of an African word, *Ipesi,* meaning Whither. He had suggested letting each letter stand for a principle in Girl Scouting—inspiration, possibilities, examples, service, ideals.

The more she mulled over the idea, the more Daisy became convinced that girls who were taught these principles would become the kind of adults needed to make and keep a better world. Furthermore, Girl Guiding would give her what she'd been looking for—a chance to participate in a worthwhile cause. What she could do she would do to the best of her ability.

Those who were closest to Daisy quit opposing her as soon as they realized she intended to go through with her plans. They readily admitted that she had one valuable asset for anyone interested in becoming a leader of girls—

she loved young people, and young people loved her. But her friends and family felt this interest in scouting would probably be short-lived.

Daisy's first step was to invite eight girls from Nina Pape's School to a tea given March 12, 1912, in the large carriage house back of her Savannah home. Right in the midst of the party she said, "I brought back something from England that I think you'll be interested in."

Looking at Daisy's warm brown eyes, sparkling with enthusiasm, the girls wondered what she was getting at. While she passed around pictures of English Girl Guides, Daisy described their sports, nature hikes and service programs. "I don't see why girls in Savannah couldn't have similar outdoor adventures and learn new skills," Daisy went on. "Would you like to form a troop?"

"Yes! Yes!" they all said eagerly.

"We'll use the carriage house for meetings," Daisy said briskly. "And my vacant lot for outdoor games."

For an hour the girls talked excitedly about their plans for their new troop. Then Daisy made them raise their right hands and solemnly promise to serve God and country, to be courteous, obedient, trustworthy, loyal and helpful. Thus was launched an organization that later would include thousands of girls in a sisterhood of service and adventure.

Using pictures of English Girl Guides for models, the Savannah troop cut, pinned, fitted and sewed their own blue uniforms. Some of them turned out so droopy and ill-fitting that Daisy was reminded of the Helpless Hands club, but the girls wore them proudly. Later, because a drab color seemed more practical for coping with Georgia clay, they changed to khaki uniforms.

For the first troop, Daisy worked out an elaborate program of activities. There were nature hikes, swimming, cookouts, trips in the launch that she gave the troop and first-aid sessions. On one occasion after the girls had bandaged one another for imaginary head wounds, fractures and sprains, they decided to show their mothers what they had learned. When they showed up at a card party where their mothers were they caused great consternation. "There's been a terrible accident," one of the mothers shrieked. It took several minutes for the girls to get their mothers calmed down and convinced that they were actually sound of limb.

Later, Daisy decided to add sports such as basketball to the program. The girls practiced on a vacant lot behind canvas curtains hung on wires, to protect them from the stares of curious or disapproving passersby. Little by little the skills and crafts for which Daisy had enthusiasm were introduced—modeling, painting, drama.

Sometime between the organizational meeting in March and the following winter, Daisy made the decision to call the movement Girl Scouting. The word scout, she thought, called to mind Indian wars, pioneers heading west, colorful personalities. For Americans it would have more flavor than the British term, Guide. The girls approved.

But then anything Daisy suggested usually met with favorable response. Scouts might tease her about her absent-mindedness or some peculiar habit such as wearing a wrist watch with only a minute hand on it, but they admired her skill and sportsmanship, which showed up whether she was engaged in an art project or outdoor cookery at a camp-out on the Savannah River. Full of ideas for masquerades, picnics or plays, she delighted her troop with shivery ghost stories and fortune telling. Under the guise of palm reading, Daisy managed to pass along many good bits of advice. The girls respected her judgment and loved her for her idealism and unselfishness.

Although Daisy sponsored a good many recreational activities, she insisted that the girls participate in good-will projects and put constant emphasis on the principle that, "A girl scout is a friend to all and helps other people at all times."

A number of girls in Savannah longed for additional troops to be organized, but many parents bitterly disapproved of girls' hiking through the woods, camping out, learning to tie knots or even being a friend to all. They believed in closely supervised ladylike activities. Sports were for tomboys. In general, adults were disinterested, amused or pessimistic, and predicted that the movement would soon collapse.

In the first humble, struggling days of Girl Scouting, Daisy carried on almost single-handed. Not content that the organization should be confined to Savannah, she wrote letters to prominent people and friends from New York to San Francisco, enlisting support. She encountered even more severe criticism of scouting than she had in Savannah—it would make for militarism and hoydenism, parents complained.

But Daisy was convinced that once people realized what Scouting would do for girls they would be in favor of it. On a one-woman crusade she spoke in community after community, trying to show how Girl Scouting prepared girls for more active, purposeful lives, how it helped those who were lonely or insecure. In some places she found troops already organized—perhaps under a local leader—claiming to be the American founder of Girl Scouting.

With gracious diplomacy, Daisy got all the troops united. She also revised the *Girl Guide Handbook,* keying it to meet the needs of American Scouts.

In 1913 Daisy opened a national headquarters in Washington, D.C. To whatever task lay at hand she brought tremendous energy, bubbling enthusiasm and a confident perseverance. Shuttling back and forth between the United States and England, she got additional information on activities and leadership.

Gradually the opposition to scouting decreased. New troops were formed across the country; activities expanded. Daisy, who had completely broken with her old way of life, now devoted all her energy and intelligence to scouting. Thinking always of what she could do for "The Girls" and where she could get help, she railroaded her friends onto committees. To excuses such as—"I'm too busy," or even to downright refusals, Daisy conveniently turned her deaf ear. "Then it's settled," she would say cheerfully. "You'll do it." Because she could dominate and still be charming, Daisy usually managed to get the cooperation she wanted, moving mountains of indifference.

At first she paid all the expenses herself. But too busy to keep figures, or perhaps incapable, she found in 1914 that more cash was needed than she had on hand. She met the emergency by selling her pearls. "Jewels are not important," she said, "the Girl Scouts are." But with more and more girls becoming scouts, the pearl money was only a stopgap. By 1915 Daisy was president of an organization that had a constitution, a national council and a membership including thousands of girls. She could no longer carry the load of supplying uniforms, badges and handbooks. To her other tasks was now added solicitation for funds. A year later the National Board of Directors, with Daisy concurring, moved the office of national headquarters to New York.

When World War I was declared, Daisy was in Scotland, where her mother had accompanied her. Immediately she plunged into Girl Guide war activities. Although she maintained her contact with Scouting at home via letter, she didn't want to lose personal touch; so she crossed and recrossed the dangerous, submarine-infested Atlantic.

As soon as the United States became involved in the war, Daisy came home. To President Wilson she sent a telegram offering the services of the Scouts. Urged by Daisy and Girl Scout leaders across the country, troops knitted sweaters which they sent overseas along with scrapbooks, gift packages and trench candles. Girl Scouts raised vegetable gardens, canned, worked at recreation centers, served as messengers in Red Cross centers, drummed, bugled and helped with Liberty Loan drives.

The Scout headquarters was swamped by requests for handbooks and equipment. Troops sprang up everywhere. Mrs. Woodrow Wilson donned a Girl Scout uniform and lent support. With selected girls, Daisy was received at the White House. Savannah paid her public tribute. Scouting had come into its own. In Hollywood Daisy appeared in an official Girl Scout picture, *The Golden Eaglet*.

After World War I, she encouraged Girl Scouts to serve their communities and their nation by performing useful tasks connected with voting, conservation, recreation, disasters and emergencies. The mushrooming growth of American scouting resulted in a widespread expansion of the movement. In 1920 the First International Conference met at Oxford, England.

Shortly after Daisy returned to America a Mr. Ledbetter, who was a wealthy Georgian, deeded the Girl Scouts a camp site on beautiful, wooded Lookout Mountain. That same year, handicapped by increasing deafness and other physical difficulties, Daisy gave up public speaking and stepped aside as president. "The only title I want from now on is that of Founder," she told the National Council. But being a friend to girls had gotten into her blood. Daisy became one of the busiest retired women in the country.

Daisy was delighted when the National Board of Directors voted to expand *The Rally* into a magazine for all girls published by the Girl Scouts and called *The American Girl*. On her travels, she enthusiastically promoted *The American Girl* and was often a contributor to its pages.

The growth of the Girl Scout movement led the National Board to realization of the need for a wise and able National Director who would give full time to the work. Such a woman they found in Jane Deeter Rippin whose vision and remarkable executive ability laid a firm foundation for the Girl Scout Organization as we know it today. Daisy was continuously at Mrs. Rippin's right hand, happy in backing up special new plans and in furthering those vital to the Girl Scouts from the first. In this Daisy showed her essential bigness of spirit.

She approved the shift from khaki uniforms, which Boy Scouts resented, to woodsy green with matching berets. And she continued her custom of sending a message to Girl Scouts on Hallowe'en—her own birthday. In one of her annual messages she quoted Arnold Bennett: " 'The deliberate cultivation of the gift of putting yourself in another's place is the beginning of wisdom in human relations.' To put yourself in another's place requires real imagination, but by so doing each Girl Scout will be able to live among others happily."

At a meeting of the National Girl Scout Committee in 1925 Daisy asked suddenly, "Why couldn't the 1926 World Camp be held in America?"

"Where could we have it?" an executive asked, looking aghast.

"Camp Edith Macy," answered Daisy, referring to a tract of land in New York recently donated to the Girl Scouts.

"We have no buildings there," someone objected.

"And no water," added another.

"Perhaps another time," someone else suggested. "Possibly in 1929."

Agitatedly Daisy pushed back an iron-gray lock of hair. "Don't put it off," she begged. "If we don't have it next year I may not be here."

The committee knew that, considering the state of her health, what she said might well be true. Besides, it was not easy to out-argue Daisy, who on occasion could be stubborn and unreasonable. They voted to rush building plans.

Day after day Daisy climbed over piles of building materials and sometimes sloshed through mud encouraging the workmen, keeping an eye on the ground-clearing, road-making and building.

Would the main hall be ready? Would the tents arrive? These and dozens of other questions plagued the executives, but Daisy, with blithe confidence, kept assuring everyone that the camp would be completed on schedule. The night before the delegates arrived everything was finished, even to the fireplace in the main hall, still smelling of fresh paint. Volunteer workers hastily distributed cots and blankets to a sea of tents surrounded by dogwood and apple blossoms.

On May 11, 1926, the delegates, led by Sir Robert and Lady Baden-Powell, rode into the camp along a drive lined with flags. Excitement reigned as brown hands clasped white hands and blue-eyed girls smiled at brown-eyed ones. That night when the delegates from thirty-one nations assembled, many were dressed in national costumes.

There were East Indian girls in softly draped saris, Japanese in silken kimonos, Czechs in embroidered skirts and blouses. On a huge fire each girl placed a fagot symbolizing her nation's gift to the world. Speaking to the delegates, Sir Robert Baden-Powell urged them, "Go from here full of the thought that you are going to promote peace and good will." At the end of the day all voices rose in:

> Day is done
> Gone the sun
> From the lakes
> From the hills
> From the sky
> All is well
> Safely rest
> God is nigh.

For Daisy it was a dream come true, and although she was in great physical pain she was radiantly happy.

Not many months later Daisy became seriously ill, but she had spiritual resources adequate to meet cheerfully

[249]

the trial of suffering. To her room in a Savannah hospital came flowers, gifts, letters from people all over the world. Daisy died January 17, 1927.

In May of 1944 a Liberty ship was launched bearing the name of Juliette Low. Living up to the indomitable courage of a woman who gave the best she had, the *Juliette Low* came through World War II unscathed. Later it was given the duty of carrying food and fuel to the hungry and homeless.

Juliette would have been proud of the ship, but even more proud of the record of Girl Scouts and Girl Guides during the war. In some countries the movement was officially forbidden. But undefeated by destruction of their headquarters, bombings and in some cases torture, girls continued to meet in cellars or in back rooms. Many as individuals, with great risk to themselves, served as couriers or participated in underground movements, struggling to keep freedom alive in their homelands.

There have been many tributes to this woman who believed in girls. On July 3, 1948, President Harry S. Truman signed the bill authorizing a three cent commemorative stamp in honor of her—one of the few ever dedicated to a woman. The city of Savannah named a school after her. Today her birthplace and childhood home is being restored as a national Girl Scout center. The scouts themselves and many people in Savannah and elsewhere are helping to collect funds, furniture and historic material.

In the last fifteen years of her life, Juliette Low achieved in Girl Scouting what for many would be a lifetime work. Mrs. Roy F. Layton, past president of the Girl Scouts of the United States of America, has this to say of her: "Probably the most remarkable thing about Juliette was her willingness to be herself. A many-sided personality, she could be artistic, generous, forthright, at times righteously indignant, but never afraid of her own convictions and feelings. Today, when our world seems so often full of uncertainty, and decisions are sometimes hard to make, Juliette Low's forthrightness reminds us that we can make progress in spite of difficulties. We tend to forget that Mrs. Low overcame all kinds of obstacles. Her deafness was a physical handicap. She had no formal training in dealing with youth, in organizing, in finance or business. Despite all, she founded an organization that has grown and flourished for more than forty years. Today her spirit still imbues Girl Scouting with her own realism, patriotism and delight in fun and adventure.

This could not have happened if Juliette Low had never wakened to the challenge that the best gift she could give was herself. She gave her time, money, energy and love to girls whom she hoped would be inspired to serve God, country, their fellow men.

The greatest tribute to Juliette Low lies not in the naming of schools, ships, funds or in commemorative stamps, but in the lives of American Girl Scouts, almost two and a half million of them, dedicated to the high ideals Juliette Low set forth one afternoon in 1912 to that little group of eight girls in Savannah.

## About the Author

Aylesa Forsee writes: "While teaching in high schools and universities and acting as counselor at a Y-Teen camp, I became deeply interested in teen-agers and their potentialities. It was inevitable after exchanging teaching for writing that I should put out a book which I hope will challenge some who read it to build the kind of life they dream about. I am not one of those writers who can point with pride to a novel or play penned at a tender age, having come into writing the long way round."

During Miss Forsee's childhood, spent mostly in Brookings, South Dakota, where her father was a physician, favorite pastimes were music, winter sports, Girl Scouting, camping and reading. Violin was her great love, but a late start made a musical career impractical. So at South Dakota State College she majored in science and social science, later picking up a Bachelor of Music degree at the MacPhail School of Music and a Master of Arts degree at the University of Colorado. Sandwiched in with teaching in Minnesota was participation in the Rochester Civic Symphony and the Duluth Symphony.

Miss Forsee's present home is in Boulder, Colorado, where she takes time out from her writing to go picnicking and camping in the Rockies and pursues her musical interest by playing in the Boulder Philharmonic Orchestra.